Sustaining Revival

Let the Visitation of God in Nagaland Spark Ours

Interviews and Text

By

C. B. NEWELL

Deep River
B O O K S

Table of Contents

Dedicated to
the Mozhüi and Murry families
with deep appreciation
for your lives in Christ
and the triumphs and struggles
you have walked through

Foreword

When I was a new believer in the 1970s someone placed a book in my hands on the Welsh Revival. While reading it, a yearning for revival was seared into my heart by the Holy Spirit. Soon I would experience a small Jesus movement revival in Ashland, Ohio. Ruined for anything else, two other men and I made a vow to seek Acts Chapter 2 no matter the cost. That vow led us to Gaithersburg, Maryland. Then in 1982 my pastor Che Ahn had a dream of a black man waving and saying, "Come to California; there's going to be a great harvest!" Twelve of us left all to follow that dream in 1984. The author and his wife, who researched and wrote this book, were among that pioneering company who came with my wife Therese and me. We fasted and prayed for revival for ten years; and then in 1994 an Acts Chapter 2 move of God swept into Pasadena and our histories were changed forever. No wonder the author is writing a history on the Nagaland Revival. Revival is inscribed in his heart, not just penned about in this book.

In 1998 I wrote a book called *Digging the Wells of Revival*, the premise of which was that where revival happened in the past it can happen again because God keeps his covenants with places and people who have moved His great heart. A young woman named Catherine Paine was my co-writer. She came from South Africa, a land richly steeped in revival history. Sometime after writing the book she felt led to take her children and spend some time back in South Africa. At one point during her journey, she found herself deep in the bush country in a little native village. She was welcomed by the chief of the village, who invited her into his hut. Amazingly, she found he was reading the very book we wrote—*Digging the Wells of Revival.* Can I hear the sound of another South African revival? The book, a seed blowing in the wind of God's providence, finds the right soil at the right time and *revival again*. That's what I'm believing for in this book on the Nagaland Revival.

Ecclesiastes 11:1 says, "Cast your bread upon the waters and after many days it will come back to you." Why should a man write a book about revival in an obscure place called Nagaland in the 1950s and again in the 1970s? I'll tell you why. When my friend casts this stirring story of a most astonishing revival upon the waters of history, it will flow through time to unimagined geographical places to reach the people or persons who will not just read but eat the word and become the broken bread of revival to a generation yet to come. The author's reward? The bread comes back to him by way of testimonies of what God did through those who read the book. Heaven attests concerning the author, "You are my instrument of revival!"

It was said of Winston Churchill that he used history like a cannon. As a young believer in Jesus, I began reading revival history and those stories exploded like a cannon within me. The angel messenger in Revelation 19:10 declared, "The testimony of Jesus is the spirit of prophecy." When the testimony of Jesus's acts in history are spoken of or written down, it releases prophetic power to recreate those acts again through prepared vessels who read and hear and by sacrifice and faith lay hold of them.

"The act of committing ink to parchment gives a deed permanence," said King Alfred. The story of the Nagaland Revival must be heard. It must be given permanence so that those who read may run. Thank you to this author for committing ink to parchment. O sons and daughters of India and the world, read and let the fire burn and faith soar. What was is what could be—and what must be again. If God is the same yesterday, today, and forever, then Nagaland is a banner to fly, a standard to rally around, and the floor, not the ceiling, from which a new generation can soar into faith for the even greater outpourings of the Spirit that are promised in the Scriptures.

In a whole region of India, almost every soul came to Christ. The pervasive presence was everywhere, mind-bending miracles were common, and plain people became portals of power from another world. Reading the stories in this book was almost shocking to me. Could I believe for this kind of revival? A dear sister in Boston heard the audible voice of God saying, "Within your womb is the greatest revival known ever to man." Boston? What if Nagaland happened in Boston? Our minds want to retreat from such a thought. Impossible. But we must not dial down the promises and dishonor the Holy One of Israel. I think every revival is an invitation to invoke the God of impossibilities made possible to act again, and this story of the Nagaland outpouring will stretch the limits of our belief "unto Him who is able to do exceeding abundantly beyond all we can think or imagine." O brothers and sisters, read the account and stir yourselves to lay hold of God and invoke the coming of the God of Nagaland!

Lou Engle
The Send
Colorado Springs, Colorado

Introduction

The Inspiration

The tall Westerner across from me didn't seem put off by my overeager request. He did take his time to answer, as if he was weighing me to see if I could handle what he had to say.

"Tell me about the revival in Nagaland!" I'd blurted out.

We were sitting in a school office similar to many such offices throughout India—more than five hundred miles from Nagaland. We had just met. I'd been told that he was familiar with the move of God there. I had an advantage over most believers from the West—as an occasional visitor to India I'd heard enough that I could at least ask a question about what happened in Nagaland. Many in the West may have heard of the Welsh revival or the Hebrides revival but have never heard of how God moved as dramatically and more recently—on the eastern border of India.

He proceeded to tell how a dozen years before, as a young man barely 20 years old, he'd been part of a Bible training program in the compound we were in. The training was led by an older man from Nagaland, known as Uncle Murry. His given name was L. Yaniethung Murry, but in his culture older men are called "Uncle" as a mark of respect.

His answer focused me on the fruit of revival in Uncle Murry's life: "He'd call a prayer meeting in the evening—and after we'd prayed from 8 to 10 p.m., he'd see us young guys falling asleep, and he'd send us off to bed.

But he'd stay up—praying and singing—and then during the night if we had to use the toilet, we'd hear him still—praying and singing." Uncle Murry had experienced something—been captured by something—that empowered a devotion I could barely picture. I was enthralled!

Perhaps my response reassured my new friend. He proceeded to relate a couple of specific examples of the move of God to show how extraordinary it was.

When Uncle Murry was young and first touched by the revival, there had been a group of scoffers, evidently in his village, who were gathered around a fire one evening making fun of the revival. A cow walked into their midst, and told them: "Jesus is coming soon. What are you doing here?" They were panic-stricken, and ran to their homes in terror—and discovered no one there because the rest of their families were at the revival service. They abandoned their scoffing and joined them!

At a different time, a group of Nepali woodcutters were working in the forest near the Naga town of Wokha and heard a hymn being sung in the trees above them. They ran into the town—to a revival service where the same hymn was being sung! Later I would hear that the Nepali church in Wokha, Nagaland traces its origin to that incident.

Then my new friend told me how Uncle Murry had first been touched by God. As a young man in the mid-1950s, Murry had walked into a church meeting. He had known he was "supposed to go"—he'd had an acquaintance-ship with the gospel from childhood. But at that service he immediately came under the conviction of the Holy Spirit, fell to the ground (like others in the room), and confessed all his sins. From there he was raised by an unseen power above the crowd on the floor—and watched the scene from mid-air.

After hearing these tidbits I couldn't shake the picture of his praying again and again, far into the night. There'd been long-term effects of his encounters with our Lord—they'd empowered lifelong devotion. Now that's revival. Even sustained revival!

This book was born out of our talk that day. Let's look together at what our Lord did in Uncle Murry and his family, in the context of a massive move of His Spirit among all the different tribes of the Nagas, a people group in the northeast part of India and northern Myanmar. By looking at examples of both how God touched people and the way this one particular family lived out their encounters with God over the years, we can get a good view of how Holy Spirit touched this area of the world. There's much for each of us to gain from their experience.

What Is Revival?

Revival.
Even using the word is challenging.

What do I mean by it—and what will others understand?

We can quickly dispose of the "wishful" or "hopeful" use of the term, when a series of special evening church meetings are called "revival meetings." We understand using the term in that way doesn't mean that "revival" is actually going on in the meetings. Yet even once we get rid of those uses of "revival," it's still a word that represents so much—and yet is so fuzzy, confusing even.

Is it "the happily ever after" of the Christian faith?

Is it about preserving something we already have? Or nostalgia about what we think we used to have?

Is it about reaching a condition, a state, that we've only imagined?

Is it a season, an event? Or a drama, a particular type of ongoing interaction of heaven and earth?

As I looked at my own motivation for seeking revival, I realize much of my desire was simple laziness. I imagined that in seasons of revival, making and teaching Jesus followers would be easy. There wouldn't be great effort involved—whether in prayer, witnessing, serving, or loving those who have yet to believe. This book will make obvious how mistaken such thinking is.

So let's clarify what we mean by "revival."

Let's look at the root of the word: *Re* = again, *vive* = life. That's simple, right? Revival must mean "bringing back to life." But generally, the word is used differently. The instances that are referred to as "revivals" from the past often involve seeing the life of God come to people who haven't been "alive" before, or seeing more life come to believers than they have ever had before.

With all that in mind, "revival," as generally used, means seeing obvious supernatural evidence of our Lord over a period of time in a community. Simply put: more of God!

There are occasions in biblical history where we see a breaking in of the Spirit of God. In addition, there is a command and a promise that indicates the possibility of revival in all generations after Christ, in all places. But this promise can easily be overlooked. Slow down and read the following sentence carefully:

> Keep your conduct among the Gentiles honorable, so that when they speak against you as evildoers, they may see your good deeds and glorify God on the day of visitation. (*1 Peter 2:12*)

This is an exhortation for all times, not simply for Peter's generation or the final generation when our Lord returns. Peter is saying that every generation can see a visitation, or a revival. The two words describe the same thing. Some English translations of this passage use the term "day of judgment," which doesn't fit with the thrust of the sentence.[1] It would be too late for unbelievers to glorify God for the conduct of His people on the day of judgment! To give a visual for the word, note that the Greek word for "visitation" is used of a military commander visiting an outpost for an inspection. To apply it in Peter's sense: the Commander has always been in charge, so His presence has been felt, but from a distance. When He visits, He's present in person.

The area inhabited by the Naga tribes (much of this area was set up as Nagaland, a state of India, on Dec. 1, 1963), experienced such a visit from

God in a series of waves during the second half of the twentieth century. We're going to look at the fruit of this visitation in one Naga family's life. Our focus allows us a more "human" view because broad narratives or statistics may not speak to our hearts as deeply as personal stories. We'll be able to see what happens as life goes on beyond revival.

Explanatory Notes

This book is for those who hunger for more of God. While I include some comments and recommendations, the bulk of the book is composed of firsthand accounts of how our Lord moved in Nagaland—letting each reader learn and reach their own conclusions.

As a disclaimer, I will note that I'm not particularly good at using binoculars. It's so frustrating to try and focus on something and end up discovering I'm off by a few degrees. Of course, then I can't see what I'd hoped to. At times this account reminds me of trying to use binoculars—how does one keep focused on what matters? I've attempted to look at revival and its fruit by studying how our Lord worked in one family over decades. However, in order to do that we need to see the overall setting as well: it took place in the midst of drastic cultural change among Naga tribes, and at the same time there were atrocities and political oppression. Trying to paint a comprehensive picture, over time, of this move of God is difficult. Still, it's worth the effort, and I trust even this sketchy view will inspire and exhilarate you!

At the same time, binoculars may focus on things we'd rather not see. This view could be called *Revival—Warts and All*. This story won't be neat and tidy. But this account will give us new clues and perspectives in the ongoing mystery thriller *Following God*. (This thriller is in fact an epic we're all personally engaged in, to some extent or another. And we never finish it this side of eternity.)

The first part of the book, through the chapter "Mission as the Fruit of Revival," contains the basics of what happened, both among the Nagas and with this particular family. This first section will share the history in broad strokes. Several topics emerge in these chapters that need more discussion—these topics are explored in the second part of the book. Here we get into details, the fine brushwork. I recognize that my immersion in this story has allowed me to think and pray through lessons to be learned and applied, so following the history in each chapter there are some comments, including possible application and reflection. Generally, this is in the form of questions or particular Bible passages to consider.

I'm saddened that part of our family's story involves disappointments with other believers in two denominations, both of which the interviewers have been part of and received from at different times in our Western context. We trust even the disappointments we find will contribute to a greater desire for unity of the Spirit in us all.

Quotations are edited at times to help Western readers understand the speaker's meaning. Words inserted [in brackets] are needed to get across the meaning; CAPITAL letters are used to show that the speaker was being emphatic. Quotations from Mhono Murry are from interviews with her in Wokha, Nagaland, October 8–11, 2019. Other interviews are footnoted.

Spelling and dates are in American English style. Pronouns used for God have been capitalized. Since Holy Spirit is both a name and a title, sometimes there will be a "the" in front, sometimes not.

Timeline

The following is provided to give a quick summary of the history covered in the book. The first section provides the narrative of the history in chronological order. The second section looks at particular topics, so different time periods may be included in one chapter.

YEAR	THE MURRY/MOZHÜI FAMILY	BROADER NAGA SOCIETY
1872		First Naga believers come from the Naga Hills and are baptized in Assam
1904	First believers in Okotso village	
1911	Merithung Mozhüi born	
1918		Naga Club—first organization connecting different tribes formed
1932	L. Yaniethung Murry born in Okotso	
1937		Start of what became Nagaland Baptist Church Council April 5

1938	Merithung goes to school in Shillong, Assam	
1944	Merithung commandeered for service by British forces	Battle of Kohima-Imphal rages through Naga territory—turning point in Asian land war
1945	Mhono Mozhüi born—May	
1947		India granted independence by British August 15; council representing Naga tribes declares independence August 14
1948		The C. E. Hunter American Baptist missionary family returns to Nagaland—November
1950		The Hunter family leaves Nagaland because of illness. C. Earl Hunter dies en route home
1951		Census: Nagaland 46.05% Christian
1952	Rikum starts ministering—eventually invited to Okotso village to preach by Pastor Phandeo—Holy Spirit moves other places as well	
1954	L. Yaniethung Murry born again in revival experience	All seven long-term U.S. missionaries ordered out by India government[2]
1955		India Army occupies Nagaland. Destruction of villages and other atrocities

1956	Merithung Mozhüi born again	
1961		Census: Nagaland 52.98% Christian; revivalists start annual conventions and networking—January
1962	Merithung selected as General Secretary of new denomination—later expelled from Bible translating center	Nagaland Christian Revival Church organizes—January
1963	L. Yaniethung (Uncle) Murry and Mhono Mozhüi wedding—December	Nagaland becomes separate state of India—December 1
1964		Nagaland Baptist Church Council plays major role in ceasefire, effective Sept. 6[3]
1965	Elizabeth Murry born— January	
1966	Thungbemo Murry born— October	
1968	Alan Murry born—August	Ao Baptists start spiritual preparation for their centennial
1970	Ajano Murry born— November	
1971		Census: Nagaland 66.76% Christian
1972	Mozhüi family founds Christian Model High School in Wokha, Nagaland; Merithung selected Secretary, Assemblies of God-Nagaland	Billy Graham meetings in Kohima, Nagaland, celebrating centennial of Naga Christianity

1974	David Murry born—July	
1975		All Nagaland Congress on World Evangelization, Dimapur, March 1–9
1976		"Revival of love" starts sweeping through Naga tribes
1977	Uncle Murry baptized in Holy Spirit—October 19	T. Alemmeren and Nagaland Baptist Church Council call for 10,000 cross-cultural missionaries, October 15
1981		Census: Nagaland 80.21% Christian
1983	Uncle Murry suspended from his government job— March 1	18 tribal Baptist associations sign 10,000 missionary covenant, April 9, 1981– November 20, 1989
1987	Uncle Murry restored to his position—May 14	
1990	Uncle Murry takes early retirement	
1991		Census: Nagaland 87.47% Christian
1992	Uncle Murry leads team to Sikkim	
1997	Mary from Bhutan adopted by the Murrys, December	
2001		Census: Nagaland 89.97% Christian

2006	Merithung Mozhüi dies	
2011		Census: Nagaland 87.93% Christian
2014	Yanasali Mozhüi, Merithung's widow, dies	

PART 1:

God's Move among the
Naga Peoples

CHAPTER 1

Surveying the Land

The LORD said to Abram . . . "Lift up your eyes and look from
the place where you are, northward and southward and east-
ward and westward, for all the land that you see I will give to
you and to your offspring forever. . . . Arise, walk through the
length and the breadth of the land, for I will give it to you."
(*Genesis 13:14–15, 17*)

Before we can focus on the personal, let's get some idea of the setting—
the context of our Naga family's story.

There are more than a dozen different Naga tribes, living in a mountainous area now divided between two political entities, India and Myanmar. The state of Nagaland was established in India in 1963, with even more
pain than a normal human birth. The state includes many but not all of the
Nagas who live in India. (The others are in the bordering states of Manipur,
Arunchal Pradesh, and Assam.) There's debate about the Nagas' roots as a
people group, but there's no question that the Nagas are completely distinct
linguistically, ethnically, and spiritually from other cultural groups in India

or Myanmar. Nagas were never followers of Hinduism, Islam, Jainism, Sikhism, or Buddhism, the predominant religions of the Indian subcontinent.

The fourteen to eighteen tribes[4] together comprise about 2.2 to 2.6 million people, a fraction of the more than 1.3 billion people now living in the political country of India.[5] The state of Nagaland is a little bigger in area than the state of Connecticut and a little smaller than the country of Kuwait or the state of New Jersey. The total territory Nagas inhabit in India would be larger than the current nation of Israel—or interestingly enough, of Wales.[6]

Starting in the 1870s, there were efforts to bring the good news to some of the Naga tribes. Seven decades of church planting and teaching brought a few of these tribes to the point of having significant Christian influence, some with as many as 50% Christian adherents.[7] This work was significant enough that the spiritual difference from other parts of the British colony could be seen when the British left. A group of Naga leaders declared independence the day before India became independent: August 15, 1947.[8] But the government of India asserted its control over all their territory. By 1954, all seven long-term missionaries were ordered out by the central government of India.[9]

Yet our Lord chose to demonstrate His power, starting during these years. Perhaps the missionaries' exit meant there was increased prayer on the Nagas' behalf. It's possible the absence of one form of teaching allowed another to blossom. Regardless, the words of Isaiah 64:3 (NKJV) can be used to describe what happened: "You did awesome things for which we did not look, You came down, the mountains shook at Your presence." Nagas are aware of the daily reality of the spiritual realm in a way most Westerners aren't. Still, they weren't looking for a replay of the day of Pentecost, nor even the signs and wonders which had occurred in a few places in India four to five decades earlier.[10] The tribes didn't have a grid or framework for believers to cry out for signs and wonders. Certainly those following Christ weren't looking for birds and animals to speak of Jesus, of buildings levitating during a prayer meeting, and of miraculous protection from bullets and grenades.

Yet all of that and more would take place—at the same time that many Nagas were or would soon be the victims of ethnic cleansing. Nagas suffered atrocities which rivaled any scorched-earth campaign in other twentieth-century wars. Yet they endured this additional ignominy: at the time, no one in the outside world knew of their fate. In our current era, with the relatively free flow of information and videos, where our major challenge is sorting and deciding what to pay attention to from the ever-flowing news glut, it's hard to comprehend that the government of India was able to simply block access and control all reporting about the area.

The initial military campaigns morphed during the 1960s into ongoing conflict and tension between independence guerrilla forces and military occupiers. Disunity in the independence movement led to disillusionment with the cause among Naga youth. Although a ceasefire in 1997 has been a functional turning point, even today the conflict isn't resolved. The Indian military are still present in large numbers.

Meanwhile, the supernatural evidence of God, the working of signs and wonders, lessened in the '60s, but some people kept the fire alive. Perhaps as importantly, there was now a basis for hunger and thirst for more of God.

This led into what Uncle Murry termed "a revival of love" in 1974 through 1977 and beyond. Or, since the effect went far beyond existing believers, we could term it "a general awakening." While the numbers of believers had been climbing steadily in the '50s and '60s, the '70s would see virtually every Naga call on the name of Jesus for salvation! Decades later, in the 2011 census of India, 88% of the population of Nagaland professed to be Christian.[11] The speed of this spiritual change caused one observer, New Zealand Bible teacher Des Short, to describe the move from Isaiah 66:8 (NKJV): "Shall the earth be made to give birth in one day? Or shall a nation be born at once? For as soon as Zion was in labor, she gave birth to her children."[12]

The evidence of God's supernatural work can be seen in statistics and church buildings, but it's also a mixed picture, with corruption and nominalism growing at the same time as other fruit. This makes under-standing revival difficult. Let's focus on one family to see if we can get a clearer picture.

Ponder and Apply

Do we need our God stories to be clear-cut, black-and-white, with no ambi-guity? Can we, in our humanness, embrace the mixture and messiness of life as it's lived?

Jonathan Edwards defended the move of God in New England in the 1730s–40s from criticism in this way:

> There being a great many errors and sinful irregularities mixed with this work of God, arising from our weakness, darkness, and cor-ruption, does not hinder this work of God's power and grace from being very glorious. Our follies and sins in some respects manifest the glory of it. The glory of divine power and grace is set off with the greater luster, by what appears at the same time of the weakness of the earthen vessel.[13]

Just because there's bad fruit along with the good doesn't mean the good didn't originate from our Lord's supernatural intervention. Can we, to use a well-worn but appropriate phrase, eat the meat and spit out the bones as we consider the Nagas' stories?

CHAPTER 2

Sowing Seeds in Fallow Ground

A sower went out to sow. (*Matthew 13:3*)

When speaking of the British occupation of the Indian subcontinent, we need to see it as an ongoing work in progress. There were various degrees of control exercised over different areas over time, some involving treaties and administrative arrangements with existing tribal or community rulers. In some regions there was occupation and direct rule by the East India Company, and eventually the British government. In addition, other European powers had territories in different parts of the Indian subcontinent (modern-day India, Pakistan, and Bangladesh).

"Work in progress" certainly described the British presence among the Naga tribes. It was only in 1832 that the British made an effort to rule this remote area and these fierce tribes. After a treaty with the king of Burma (modern-day Myanmar) gave Britain authority over the areas of Assam and Manipur, the British needed to connect these areas—which involved invading the territory of different Naga tribes. So the Naga Hills, as they were generally known, became British-ruled—although not completely.

The terrain was so mountainous and the tribes so fierce that the British were content to leave about half the area of what is now the state of Nagaland outside the British Empire's functional authority.

The apostle Thomas reached India, and there are groups which trace their spiritual lineage to his work. Believers of both the Roman Catholic and Eastern Orthodox traditions have been present for centuries in the subcontinent. But all of these were far away from the lands of the Nagas. The process of getting the gospel to the Nagas began with Protestant missionaries coming during the British occupation. Particularly in the beginning, there was an uneasy relationship between the colonizers and the missionaries, who after all were ambassadors for different kings. One example was that in the 1790s, *British Baptist William Carey couldn't legally preach in any territory ruled by the British East India Company.* Because of this, in 1800 he moved his work outside the British-ruled city of Kolkata to nearby Serampore, which was governed by Denmark. Carey is generally seen as the pioneer who did the most to spark the Protestant mission movement.

Eventually this mission movement would reach the Nagas, starting in 1839. There was tension here with the British colonial officials as well. Americans Edward and Mary Clark, who led the initial gospel breakthrough among the Nagas reported that cruel customs which their preaching had ended in some villages were then encouraged by British government officials.[14]

Again, in telling about this move of God among the Nagas, much of the focus in this book will be on one family and one tribe. However, to help give the context of this remarkable history, there will be some sense of the larger picture. By using their own words, you as the reader can catch firsthand the feelings and perspective of those who've encountered and sustained a visitation of God. In this vein, here's an account by American Baptist[15] missionary Robert B. Longwell of his early visits to Okotso village of the Lotha tribe, written several years after his initial visit in 1904.[16] This is our Naga family's home village, so his visits are part of the work which leads to them encountering Christ. Okotso would become a center of the Holy Spirit's work in the 1950s:

> I had been in the village of Okotso twice—once in the year 1907 and again in 1908. On the second occasion I had met with some resistance on the part of the village chief. He knew that I was not a Government official, and that I represented the new custom which had barely been introduced into his community. Several boys from his village had trained in our Impur[17] Mission School, and when they returned to their own people they naturally told about the new custom which they themselves had accepted. They had told this story with an enthusiasm and a delight which was infectious and the result was that a few of the Lothas in the village of Okotso, perhaps a dozen, had accepted Christianity. I asked the old chief in as kindly a spirit as I could and pretending [not] to notice the negativity he had displayed to me, if he would be willing to tell me why he was opposed to the teaching of Christianity in his village. He very freely and frankly stated his conviction that the new custom was both good and right and that in the course of time it would be accepted by all the local residents, but he had decided that they should not accept it in his generation. That seemed like a fairly good place to stop the conversation.

Longwell then told how a year later he came to the village for a third time at the request of the believers there. They had asked him to come to baptize a number of new believers; evidently Longwell, like most leaders in his era, hadn't taught about the authority of all believers to water-baptize, and the importance of doing it promptly. They were planning on doing the baptisms in the evening. Longwell knew there were other villagers intent on persecuting the new believers, so he persuaded them to do the baptisms in an out-of-the-way "little nook," while the rest of the village were out in the fields. When he returned to the village, he noticed a small group of a dozen men in intense conversation, but didn't think anything of it. Their numbers kept growing throughout the afternoon, as he waited for the time to begin the preaching and communion service. (Although he doesn't say explicitly why he wanted the water baptisms to be done earlier than the preaching service, it's likely that he thought the baptisms would be more provocative to those persecuting the faith. Water baptisms meant their own tribespeople were making a public profession of faith, as opposed to an outsider like himself simply speaking.) The time for starting the meeting passed and no one showed up. In fact, two more hours went by:

> The crowd at the upper end of the village now numbered about a hundred and was decidedly noisy. At this moment [his host Ichungo] showed himself at my tent and suggested that the evening meeting be omitted. I asked for an explanation. He then told me he had overheard the plans that were developing at the head of the village. He said that the crowd had decided on a program the first act of which was to take the missionary's head. The second act was to take his. . . . The third was to take the head of Etisassao,[18] the most influential Christian in the village, and one who, indeed, had done more than any other to start the little church. The last number of this unusually interesting program was to light upon the Christians as a body and cut to pieces all who did not escape to the jungle. At this juncture it dawned upon me that it was time to move.

Longwell, writing well after the event, told the story with humorous deliberation, but no doubt there were anxious moments during the actual events:

> I immediately called my cook, Paniwalla, two boys I had with me from the Impur school, and the few Christians who were in sight, and asked them if they thought we had better leave the village. They gave me the comforting assurance that I might take whatever course I chose but as for them they were going to leave the village without delay.

He asked the believers *if they had time*, could they take down the tent and pack things before fleeing the village. Then Longwell went on:

Just at that moment the crowd at the head of the village called out announcing their decision which was exactly as related to me by the teacher. I went into the tent, dropped to my knees and asked for guidance that I might do the right thing in this emergency. When I arose from prayer I was aware that the mob had moved down to the tent and were so close to it as to be interfering with the cords of it. I picked up my new double-barrelled shotgun, put [in] two cartridges and went out of the tent. I found it surrounded on all sides except in front where my own company stood. The only way out of the village was to file out past the mob. I felt my chief responsibility was for the two school boys I had taken with me. . . . I asked them if they would follow me. They said they would. I cocked both hammers of my gun and with fingers on both triggers and carrying the piece at an angle which brought the muzzle just above the heads of the rabble, I left the village and the two boys and a few others . . . accompanied me.

Longwell and his group got outside the village about an eighth of a mile, and then decided to stop and wait down a side path. The drama continued:

In a short time the two chief men of the village came and pretended to be friendly. . . . They began to urge us to return to the village and gave as their reason certain statements which it would take too long to relate but which I utterly discounted. My own conclusion was that they were afraid of being reported to officers of the British Government and severely punished. . . . While they parleyed, the Christians kept coming up one by one bringing with them the tent and the things we had left in the village, until finally all had arrived except my cook (Kinūkaba) who although an Ao Naga, was able to speak and understand the Lotha language. Ultimately he came up and by that time the chief men from the village had almost persuaded us to return on the promise that no further trouble would be given us.

When the cook came up we asked what he thought about . . . this promise. He repeated the generous assurance that I might return if I cared to but as for him he was going on to the first village of his own tribe, and he said that as he was leaving the village just now the last thing he heard was the sound of people sharpening their "noks" and he heard them say "If we do not get them tonight we will get them on the path in the morning."

So the entire group proceeded to hike through the night in the moonlight. Their journey through the mountains involved some rest breaks, including one for a time of prayer. By this time, Longwell was famished, and the grape juice he'd taken for the communion service was the only nourishment he had with him. He said it "was the rarest beverage I ever tasted, and as the supply was so limited I allowed myself only a swallow or two at a time." They finally arrived at the Ao village of Longkhüm[19] about 4:00 a.m. His sleep was "sweet and refreshing indeed." Longwell closed the story, noting: "Today the church at Okotso has a membership of about a hundred. . . . Many of their former persecutors are now numbered among the Christians."[20]

We need to include the Okotso Baptist Church's account of the aftermath as well. It will give some indication of the "messiness" of mission work. Their history includes a detail Longwell doesn't mention; when the chieftains came and tried to persuade them to come back to the village, they brought a rooster with them to try and appease the fleeing missionary. Longwell reported the incident to the British official in charge of the area, who ordered the villagers to identify the culprits who plotted to kill Longwell. But no one would confess and testify against anyone else, so the official imposed five hundred hours of forced labor. This caused some of the villagers who were punished to decide they should become Christians to avoid future punishment. The church's history concludes: "Subsequently 30 households became Christians just for the sake of escaping punishment, but the hand of the Lord was at work and they became staunch believers."[21]

Thus we see how, thanks to the Longwells—and of course, their companions on the field and the "senders" who kept them on the field—the church at Okotso can trace its origins to 1904.

The missionary effort no doubt lost steam as Japanese ambitions to conquer Asia became apparent in the late 1930s. World War I had involved a couple of thousand Nagas going to Europe to help fight in a distant war— but World War II would come directly to their soil. The land of the Nagas became the strategic entry point for the Japanese to invade India from Burma.

Ponder and Apply

Picture yourself not as Longwell, but as a member of an American Baptist church in your community, giving to the missions' offerings faithfully in the early 1900s. You may not even have a personal awareness or connection with a "go-er," like the Longwells. Your prayers may be perfunctory—"Lord, bless our missionaries."

Yet somehow, those efforts would eventually yield fruit, no doubt far beyond even the imagination of the Longwells, as Okotso would become a key site for the visitation of the spirit of our Lord!

What are you sowing into now that could eventually grow far beyond your imagination? Are you sowing with the expectancy there will be a harvest—not for your gain, but heaven's?

CHAPTER 3

World War Enters Our Story

Other seeds fell among thorns, and the thorns grew up and choked them. Other seeds fell on good soil and produced grain, some a hundredfold, some sixty, some thirty. (*Matthew 13:7–8*)

The missionary impulse led to the founding of many schools and hospitals in the Indian subcontinent—including the region now called Northeast India. A school headmaster with missionary zeal and a deep heart for the Lord played a crucial role in our family's story; he touched one patriarch of the family whose history we'll follow. This patriarch was Merithung Mozhüi, born in 1912 to a family of poor farmers in the Lotha village of Lungstung. Although he was water-baptized as a youth, he wasn't a believer and had no knowledge of the Christian faith when he went some three hundred miles away to a secondary level school in Shillong, Assam, at age 26 in 1938. "While in the High School, Reverend Pugh, his headmaster taught him proper message about Jesus, whose teaching had tremendous influence on his faith in later years." [22]

Merithung's second daughter Mhono, now married to L. Yaniethung "Uncle" Murry, told how Merithung was influenced—and how it was done with a passion that doesn't fit our general understanding of "stiff upper lip" British reserve. William Pugh, the missionary-minded headmaster of the school in Shillong, was upset that Merithung wasn't coming to Sunday school, so he had one of his fellow students go and call Merithung. The student called him again and again, but Merithung still wouldn't come to Sunday school. So Pugh told the student to just carry him on his back. This was easier said than done, as Merithung was more than six feet tall. When the student told Merithung he was going to carry him, Merithung gave in: "Okay—then I will come. Why should you carry me? I will come." Mhono said the headmaster "asked so many questions, but my father couldn't answer" because he didn't know anything about the Bible. The headmaster "started crying, and then he did a special class for my father, teaching him the Bible. . . . Then my father could pick up ALL the Bible stories." However, he still didn't become a believer.

Merithung's character and temperament were shown by the way he left school—his brother died, and it confronted Merithung with questions about what he was doing with his life. So he burned all his books, left school, and went back to his village—a journey of both great physical and cultural distance.

Yet even in the remote Naga Hills, international politics would touch his life. Japan was invading the continent of Asia in a number of places as the 1940s began, and eventually conquered British-controlled Burma in 1942 to the south of the Naga Hills. But Japanese ambitions didn't stop at Burma; from Burma the Japanese launched an invasion into India. Their invasion aimed to go through the mountains of the Naga territory in order to reach the plains of Assam and Bengal and eventually to take one of the key cities of the entire British Empire, Kolkata.

Kohima, which would become the capital of the Indian state of Naga-land, is located at a narrow pass through a mountain range. The battle for it, although not well known, has been termed "The Stalingrad of the East"—the key turning point in this entire theater of the war.[23] It was the first place the Japanese Imperial Army was defeated in their multipronged invasion of the Asian mainland:

At the height of Battle of Kohima, as troops under the dogged Colonel Hugh Richards fought the Japanese virtually eyeball-to-eyeball over the deputy commissioner's[24] tennis court, aircraft were ferrying artillery, ammunition, food and fresh troops as near to the hill town as they possibly could. Even then, it was extremely hard work to supply Kohima. Water was pumped into the inner tubes of . . . tires and dropped to the dehydrating troops from C-47 Dakotas flying just above tree height, in clear range of enemy guns. During the height of the battle, fought in temperatures 100 degrees Fahrenheit and into the monsoon, the water ration for the defenders of Kohima actually rose from one to three vital pints a day.

The Japanese fought tenaciously at Kohima, but quite simply ran out of everything. At the beginning of the battle, though, an Allied victory was far from assured. A motley garrison of some 3,500 soldiers (some accounts give a figure as low as 1,200 and, of these, just 500 are said to have been crack troops) faced between 12,000 and 15,000 seasoned Japanese soldiers. . . . One private at the height of the siege had asked Colonel Richards, "When we die, sir, is that the end, or do we go on?"[25]

Merithung was touched by the war. It turned out well, but could have ended very differently. He was some distance away from Kohima, nearer to the town of Wokha, where some British were burying some of their dead. When his daughter Mhono, who was born just after the war, told the story, she described how Merithung was "caught" by British soldiers. But his education in Shillong saved him from other duties or a different fate. The British soldiers were so impressed by Merithung's command of "the King's English," since most Nagas spoke at best broken English, that they put him in charge of a food storehouse in Wokha. Mhono's future father guarded the storehouse well, not touching a single item of the inventory. When the British soldiers returned, they rewarded him by giving him a great number of different canned foods. Mhono recalled with laughter what happened when Merithung took those home to his family: his wife Yanasali didn't like canned goods, so the couple gave them all away.

The Allied forces' death toll of 4,064 for the Battle of Kohima was greater than the number of the original garrison. The battle raged from April 4 to June 22, 1944. The battle monument erected alongside the tennis court at Kohima reads:

When you go home tomorrow, tell them of us and say

For your tomorrow, we gave our today.[26]

One commentator sprang off of that epitaph to point out the irony of what followed, particularly in terms of the Nagas:

What sort of tomorrow those who fell at Kohima were fighting for was, however, difficult to say even then. In a little more than three years, the British were gone, not just from Kohima and the Naga Hills, but from the whole of the subcontinent. As for the Nagas, Kohima was a proud moment of sorts, but they were soon to be subject to a new form of imperialism, neither British nor Japanese, but Indian.[27]

Eight years after the battle a wave of revival would begin among the Lotha tribe. About twelve years after helping the British soldiers, and eighteen years after his headmaster's tears, Merithung actually started following our Lord Jesus. Mhono tells about her father coming to faith. It wasn't a dramatic moment in one of the revival meetings that had been going on in some villages for a couple of years—it happened as he was walking along one morning to his office. She described him feeling the devil tell him in his heart, "Jesus is not God." After that, she said, "Suddenly the word that headmaster told him while he was in the school came to his mind: 'Oh, my headmaster Bill is an Oxford product, a highly educated person. Even he taught me that Jesus is the Son of God! Then why are you tempting me like that?' He rebuked the devil, like that."

Merithung's booklet adds some details. Prior to this spiritual confrontation, Merithung had two significant dreams:

Some day in March—April 1954, I had a strange dream. In the dream I saw a big and shining eye flashing on me from heaven. I was running away and hiding myself from the eye. I hid myself in a cave, but it could not save [me] from the shining eye. I ran away from the cave and hid myself in the hollow of a big tree, but it could not save me from the searching light of God. Then I got tired of running away from the eye of God. And I was caught. I woke up sighing.

Several years[28] before I was converted I had a very strange dream. In the dream I was a pilgrim, walking along the ridge of a long mountain range. On either side of the narrow footpath along which I was walking there were roaring tigers, and the region was said to be a dangerous one. I reached the place where there was a small platform made of wooden planks. As I stood on the platform it broke into two pieces and I fell into a narrow pit which I understood was a bottomless one. I was falling deeper and deeper and had no hope of surviving from the fall.

Then suddenly I thought of God and started crying out continuously saying "But there is God! But there is God!" As I was repeating these words I was gently thrust out of the pit and found myself crucified against a brick wall in a terrible agony. . . . When I lifted my eyes, I saw a small group of people, mostly of women, in front of me, sitting on benches in a meadow. In front of the people was a small table with a Bible and hymn book on itself. A man stood up from among the people and said to me saying "Merithung what are you doing there? Come down and lead the Lotha Association."[29] I replied "No, I cannot do that, for I can neither pray, preach or sing."

The man entreated me three times: but I refused saying the same thing. At last he got annoyed at my refusal and said angrily "Even if you cannot pray, preach or sing it does not matter." I felt sorry for annoying him and said, "All right." As soon as I agreed to his wish I was loosened from the cross. I stood in front of the table and began preaching the word of God. I woke up joyfully with much sweat. I wondered what manner of dream I just had.[30]

Merithung's account of his coming to Christ concludes:

On that particular morning in 1956, the Devil tried his best to deceive me, but by the grace of God it turned out to be an opportunity for me to confess that Jesus is the Son of God. Yes, 1 John 4:15 says: "Whoever shall confess that Jesus is the Son of God, God dwells in him and he in God." The precious tears shed by my respected teacher did not go in vain; those tears bore fruit eighteen years later on that morning.[31]

Ponder and Apply

Am I good soil? Is there good soil around me? Nagas in World War II experienced the turmoil and even the terror of being near an invading army's path. There was also ambiguity that could confuse their responses: "Were the Japanese a liberating army?" Similar events can tenderize hearts today. But outside turmoil doesn't necessarily disturb the stony ground of human hearts—unless there's been spiritual preparation. The most profound spiritual fruit in this account came sometime *after* the war, even after the political change of rulers from London to New Delhi—but from seeds sown long before.

It's appropriate at this point to give an observation from another move of God. J. Edwin Orr, arguably one of the greatest students of revivals and a seminary professor who taught and wrote extensively on the subject, "came to the conclusion towards the end of his life that 'the

Awakening of 1857–58 was the most thorough and wholesome movement ever known in the Christian Church.'"[32] The name most associated
with this move of God is Jeremiah Lanphier, who started a noon prayer
meeting on September 23, 1857 at the North Reformed Dutch Church
building in New York City.

> The first week only six attended. The next week the number reached
> twenty and the following, forty. During October, the meetings pre-
> viously held weekly, became daily. (Oct. 14 there was a general
> financial collapse shaking all classes in the city). By the time the new
> year began a second room had to be used simultaneously to accom-
> modate the numbers and in February a third. By then a number of
> similar meetings had begun elsewhere in the city and so marked
> was the turning to prayer that the *Daily Tribune* of 10 February
> 1858, reported, "Soon the striking of the five bells at 12 o'clock will
> generally be known as the 'Hour of Prayer.'" . . . [Lanphier's pastor, J.
> W. Alexander, reported:] "The openness of thousands to doctrine,
> reproof, etc., is undeniable. Our lecture is crowded unendurably—
> many going away. The publisher of Spurgeon's sermons, says he has
> sold a hundred thousand." . . . by June figures of 50,000 conversions
> in New York and 200,000 across the northeast were in circulation.[33]

But a key observation of what happened in this particular move of God,
illustrated by Merithung's testimony, is Pastor Alexander's observation in
a private letter that most of the new members added to their church during this revival were *chiefly* "persons with whom I have been dealing for
years."[34] A visitation can be when seeds which have been sown and watered
for months and years suddenly sprout—all at once!

Did British missionary William Pugh see in his headstrong student
Merithung Mozhüi a future revival leader, missionary, and evangelist?
What's the equivalent for us?

CHAPTER 4

Revival Happens Personally

They said to each other, "Did not our hearts burn within us while He talked to us on the road, while He opened to us the Scriptures?" (*Luke 24:32*)

. . . the eunuch saw him no more, and went on his way rejoicing. (*Acts 8:39b*)

Up to this point in our Naga family's story we can see evidence of the supernatural work of our Lord, but would we label it revival?

Maybe not. Perhaps this is because much of our view of revival may focus on a whole church being affected, or a large portion of a community being touched. Yet at its core, the supernatural work of God must be personal—His visitation must affect individuals and households. Then, when there are "enough" of those individual and family visitations, others start to notice and say: God is moving!

Let's continue our account of God's supernatural work among the Nagas by looking at what happened to another, younger man from the same village, in 1952. The two would end up closely connected in our Lord's work.

L. Yaniethung Murry came to the Lord before Merithung, and at a much younger age. As this book is being written he's now advanced in years. It's customary in much of the Indian subcontinent to refer respectfully and affectionately to men older than one's self as "Uncle," so we'll refer to him as "Uncle Murry." This is particularly appropriate in the case of L. Yaniethung Murry, both because of his age (he was born in 1932), and because his heart of love is so apparent to anyone. His youngest son David says of him, "Where I would have crucified somebody (after a conflict), my dad would embrace that person. He had something more than compassion—he discerned something in people—very much like God."

Uncle Murry was the second-born of an often absent and frequently drunk father, in the small village of Okotso in 1932. There had been believers there for almost three decades, as the village had been reached by missionaries early in the twentieth century.[35] There ended up being eight children in Yaniethung's family. In his own words, "The Lord of Lords raised and protected me through hunger and thirst."

His wife Mhono says: "God has chosen certain people—from [their] mother's womb. So my husband also, he must be a chosen of God, because he suffered SOOOOOO much when he was young. He contracted dysentery and there was no cure. His mother was also very poor and so his mother could not take care of him. One night he ALMOST died." But a man in the village had a dream where he saw an angel saying he was going to visit Yaniethung. The villager thought that meant Yaniethung would die, so he went to visit the family first thing in the morning to console them. Instead, he found that Yaniethung was improving—the angel's visit had brought healing!

Somehow in the midst of his family's financial lack, Yaniethung was able to pursue schooling. In 1952 he had gone with his class to the larger town (and future capital of Nagaland state) Kohima for exams.

At this point, let's give more details to his story we heard at the beginning of the book. When he returned, a supernatural visitation was underway and there was a meeting at the village Baptist church building. He'd led a nominal Christian life up to this point. In fact, when he had walked home from his own water baptism as a youth, he'd stolen firewood from a neighbor! However, when Yaniethung entered that worship service after his exams, he had a spiritual encounter and fell to the ground, confessing his sins. Then an unseen force lifted him from the ground, and he was able to look down on the scene of others who were also confessing and crying out to the Lord.

This encounter, part of a larger move of God which touched other Naga tribes, permanently marked him. We see his conversion as supernatural—an act of revival. Yet, was it any more supernatural than Merithung's two dreams, followed by what could be seen as an internal mental struggle to act upon what he'd been taught years earlier? Any experience of salvation indicates personal revival. Still, let's give a fuller version of another story we briefly shared earlier. This is from that period in the early 1950s in Okotso—and shows the level of supernatural activity:

> There was a group of older people whose hearts were kind of hardened, and they were not yet a part of the revival that was going on in the church, it was like a year or two of meetings, day in and day out. And this group of older men were sitting around the fire at night and they were kind of mocking those who were in the church. A cow put his head in the circle, between them, and said, "Jesus is coming. What are you doing here?" They looked at each other in bewilderment and fear, "Have I gone crazy?" They saw that everyone heard the same thing! In fear, they ran to their homes, finding no one there because they were all in church. Being afraid, being alone, they ran to the church. And there was such a mighty presence of God that they confessed and they shared what had just happened.[36]

Ponder and Apply

An account of the visitation of God in Argentina over the last two decades of the twentieth century gives us this summary about the nature of revival:

> Historically the average duration of a widespread revival is just several years. Mortals wear down. Prosperity sets in because of the blessings of God and the upward lift of the gospel. People find they need time for . . . everyday affairs. So all-night prayer vigils and late-night services are out of the question. Meeting at the church [building] for prayer at five o'clock [in the morning] seems ludicrous. The revival turns into a bittersweet memory rather than something to be lived. It becomes impractical to continue.
>
> Quite a number of Welsh immigrants live in southern Argentina. Hard economic times in their own land combined with the guidance of the Holy Spirit to send them to the sheep herding lands of Patagonia [part of Argentina]. Many of the people still tell stories that were passed down about the revival in Wales in 1904, and it wasn't so long ago that the old men used to get together and reminisce in melancholy tones about those amazing days. However, even this famous revival only lasted three years.
>
> So why has this present move of God lasted for more than twenty years in Argentina? Some would say that it only exists in three or four well-known churches and that the revival has actually been over for quite a while. But the pastors don't really see it that way. They know God is at work in their churches.[37]

Uncle Murry's story, as well as the larger history of God's move in Nagaland—or Argentina—ask us to look at our own lives and ponder our own

personal revivals. Each of us has had encounters with the Spirit of God—
and just as importantly, each of us can in the future. Are we living up to what
we've experienced? Are we hungering for more? Is there something specific
quenching our thirst for God?

> Only let us live up to what we have already attained.
> (*Philippians 3:16, NIV*)

CHAPTER 5

Horror Starts after Revival Begins

And alas for women who are pregnant and for those who
are nursing infants in those days! Pray that your flight may
not be in winter or on a Sabbath. For then there will be great
tribulation. (*Matthew 24:19–21a*)[38]

After our Lord started touching people in Okotso village, other Nagas
began to suffer atrocities. One history records that when the soldiers of
"the Assam Rifles entered the Naga Hills in 1954, they began to pervasively
commit heinous crimes against the Naga populace."[39] The central government
of India had decided to stop the Naga independence movement by
force. The Naga people culturally had little in common with India, and both
their leadership and the population at large wanted independence.[40] Prime
Minister Nehru, on the other hand, had no intention of allowing the Nagas
to be independent of the newly created nation-state of India.

March 31, 1955, the Naga National Council (NNC—the independence forces) sent the following telegram to the United Nations:

Reports reaching Kohima say that more than ten thousand men, women and children of Free Nagas are believed to have been already killed by the Indian troops within the last few days of wholesale massacre. People are being butchered systematically from village to village in Free Nagaland. We urgently appeal to you in the name of humanity to intervene and stop the killings.

The U.N. failed to respond. . . . Six months after the NNC's telegraph reached the U.N., the Indian Army moved into Nagaland officially with two divisions, and "the horror and nightmare of Nagaland multiplied a hundredfold." Thousands of people were slaughtered like helpless animals. It made no difference whether the victims were combatants or civilians, men, women, children or babies.[41]

Simply mentioning numbers really doesn't convey the horror of the time, nor the incredible stress which affected Nagas wherever they lived. We'll look at a few individual instances later in the book to help fill out the picture of the times surrounding this revival. There is a sense that Naga society as a whole has post-traumatic stress disorder.

But one point should be made now: these atrocities were carried out with almost no outsiders knowing. Nagas didn't flee to a nearby country, as many would-be victims of genocide have been able to do. The philosophical question "If a tree falls in the forest without anyone hearing, does it make a noise?" becomes poignant. If a village disappears and no one (beyond the assailants) knows—did it happen?

Ponder and Apply

The link between a visitation of God being followed by horrific tragedy isn't uniform throughout history—but there are other instances. The birth of the church, followed by the destruction of Jerusalem in AD 70, is a precedent. Another would be the awakening of 1857–58 mentioned two chapters earlier, mainly associated with New York City. That awakening actually affected many parts of the United States—shortly before the whole of the United States would descend into civil war. Of course, along with that soon-coming tragedy, a spur to that spiritual awakening was the general financial collapse of October 1857. As a balance to the focus on New York City and the northeast, it's worth mentioning an example of visitation outside the northeast, in the heart of what would become the Confederacy—which includes a comment on the pattern of revival preparing for tragedy. This move took place in Zion Church, a mainly African American church, in Charleston, South Carolina, led by Dr. John Girardeau:

> Here also in 1858 special prayer meetings were begun "that constantly increased until the house was filled. At that point some of Girardeau's church officers counseled the starting of special preaching services, but "he steadily refused, waiting for the outpouring of the Holy Spirit." . . . Then, at one of these evening prayer meetings the preacher received the most distinct conviction that their prayers were heard and he announced, "The Holy Spirit has come; we will begin preaching tomorrow evening." But when the congregation was dismissed they would not depart, nor did they till Girardeau had proclaimed Christ to them until midnight. "A noted evangelist from the North, who was present, said, between his sobs, to an officer of the church: 'I never saw it in this fashion.'" Girardeau spoke of what began that night as "the most glorious work of grace I ever felt or witnessed. It began with a remarkable exhibition of the Spirit's supernatural power. For eight weeks, night after night, I preached to dense and deeply moved congregations." Even when the revival itself was over, he writes, "The work grew steadily until it was arrested by the war." As with so many others, he always believed that this great ingathering was the merciful work of God prior to the conflict [the U.S. Civil War started in 1861] which was so soon "to sweep so many of them into eternity."[42]

This move of the Holy Spirit in Charleston wasn't isolated. *The Presbyterian Magazine* for June 1858 spoke of 200,000 conversions in the southern states during this season—matching what was reported in the Northeast.[43] The 1858 United States situation and the Nagaland situations aren't precisely parallel, but we can see, like Mhono does, that the mercy of God was reaching many Nagas before they encountered death, injury, or devastation at the hands of the central government of India.

The Nagas' experience also raises the question: How does a believer engage in public life, in civil society? As a believer, would you join the independence forces?

Injustice, whether historical or current—or even anticipated in the future—forces us to trust God. It also offers us the opportunity to cry out to Him—to join in some way the dynamic which the apostle John saw:

> I saw under the altar the souls of those who had been slain for the word of God and for the witness they had borne. They cried out with a loud voice, "O Sovereign Lord, holy and true, how long before you will judge and avenge our blood on those who dwell on the earth?" (*Revelation 6:9–10*)

Injustice can also test us—do we really believe prayer is the most important priority?

> The Christian who prays acts more effectively and more decisively on society than the person who is politically involved, with all the sincerity of faith put into the involvement. It is not a matter of seeing them in opposition to one another, but of inverting our instinctive, cultural hierarchy of values.[44]

At the same time, it will test whether we're praying for our will—our idea of justice—or the will of our Lord, who manages to bring justice and mercy together through one sacrificial action. The martyrs under the altar in John's vision of heaven were given a sobering answer that may offend our hearts and our minds:

> Then they were each given a white robe and told to rest a little longer, until the number of their fellow servants and their brothers (and sisters) should be complete, who were to be killed as they themselves had been. (*Revelation 6:11*)

This answer to the martyrs ties into what Paul says: that he longs to share in Jesus' sufferings (Philippians 3:10). Paul says something even more intriguing in his letter to the Colossians—that there's still something to come in terms of Christ's afflictions and suffering:

> Now I rejoice in my sufferings for your sake, and in my flesh I am filling up what is lacking in Christ's afflictions for the sake of His body, that is, the church. (*Colossians 1:24*)

May we have the grace to embrace the trio John starts the book of Revelation with: "I, John, your brother and partner in the tribulation and the kingdom and the patient endurance that are in Jesus" (Revelation 1:9). There's suffering—and kingdom (glory, majesty, and rulership)—as we persevere. We can see the two dynamics of kingship and suffering being brought together in Romans 8:

> The Spirit himself bears witness with our spirit that we are children of God, and if children, then heirs—heirs of God and fellow heirs with Christ, provided we suffer with him in order that we may also be glorified with him. . . . Who shall separate us from the love of Christ? Shall tribulation, or distress, or persecution, or famine, or nakedness, or danger, or sword? As it is written, "For your sake we are being killed all the day long; we are regarded as sheep to be slaughtered." No, in all these things we are more than conquerors through him who loved us. (*Romans 8:16–17, 35–37*)

This isn't to say any particular visitation of God will be followed by bloodshed, or to suggest that the amount of blessing will in some way parallel the amount of suffering. But the move of the Holy Spirit in Nagaland in the '50s does need to be seen in the framework of the tragedy the Naga people would go through.

CHAPTER 6

How Does Revival Start?

Do not marvel that I said to you, "You must be born again."
The wind blows where it wishes, and you hear its sound, but
you do not know where it comes from or where it goes. So it is
with everyone who is born of the Spirit. (*John 3:7–8*)[45]

Jesus's answer to Nicodemus's question about what it means to be born
again, or born by the Spirit, makes clear that our chapter title is unan-
swerable. Evidently we can't know where revival comes from. But yet, like
Nicodemus, we want to understand!

Besides desperate circumstances, what seedbed germinates revival?

Does extraordinary prayer always precede revival? Or proceed from
revival?

The initial move of God in Nagaland is striking in that it occurred
among church groups which had no grid or framework for tangible Holy
Spirit activity. God did awesome things that weren't looked for! There
doesn't appear to have been a significant movement of prayer in Okotso
before our Lord supernaturally touched the village.[46] The prayer that is
mentioned was elsewhere, in another tribe!

This beginning of supernatural interventions in Okotso village can be seen from a couple of perspectives. It fits the view that supernatural manifestations of our Lord can be passed on from one anointed person to another—through the laying on of hands, or at least physical proximity and direct contact. Mhono Murry said Rikum Ao (his last name is the same as his tribe's name) went to study theology in Allahabad, India and there received "Holy Spirit fire" from someone's ministry. He "came back to Nagaland and started working miracles in Nagaland."

Rikum was preaching in both Longkhüm and Mangmetong villages, which are Ao tribe villages near Okotso, a Lotha tribe village. Mhono said that Okotso villagers went to the neighboring villages: "They went and saw the working of the Holy Spirit and so, so many people rejected this preacher, but our Okotso village people, they went and saw and heard the word, and they found everything to be all right, so they accepted it. And he came to Okotso village to preach revival, so the whole village got revived."

Chunbeno Murry, Uncle Murry's youngest sister, remembers the events as a young child of 4–5 years old. She said the Lotha tribespeople in Okotso watched what was happening among the Ao tribe in the village next to theirs: "So what happened to these Mangmetong people? We never see them coming and working in the fields? What happened to them?" Since all villagers depended upon their work in the fields for their food, they were quite curious what was causing them to neglect their fields. Eventually, she said, four Lotha ladies from Okotso were sent to "spy." She thinks the Lotha villagers watched the revival meetings of the Ao village for two years before deciding this move was of the Lord and in line with the Bible! Then they invited it to their town.[47]

Rikum's ministry was attacked in his home tribe. Mhono said he was called "Satan" in one Ao village, and they wouldn't accept him. "There was a BIG gum tree, a rubber tree, he even let the rubber tree fall down and raised it up. He even did that and showed it to the villagers, but they did not believe. He spoke what Jesus did, he did what Jesus did in the Bible, but the village did not accept him, so he came to Okotso village."

Rikum and a fellow revival leader Toshi experienced a number of supernatural manifestations:

On July 12, 1952 evangelist I. Toshi was passing through a deep forest on his way on a preaching trip. In the middle of the road, a tiger was devouring its prey—a cow. He commanded the tiger in the name of the Almighty God to give way and the tiger calmly moved down the other side of the road, leaving the carcass behind. After passing by, as he turned back, the tiger was seen roaring and devouring the cow again.

This seems to be a taste of the fulfillment of Isaiah's prophecies about the coming of the Messiah. He speaks of lions and leopards changing their ways and that animals will "not hurt or destroy in all my holy mountain" (Isaiah 11:9). Hosea 2:17–18 also speaks of God making a covenant for people with the beasts of the field—implying no more enmity, as part of the new day that's coming. Here's another of Toshi's adventures:

In Mangmetong village, while he was walking on the street with evangelist Rikum, he saw two angels leading their way. He asked whether Rikum could see something above. He smiled and told him that in fact he was waiting for Toshi to tell him whether he too saw the two angels leading them.

Besides angelic guidance, our Lord also spoke in another way to Ao tribe member Toshi, to go to a neighboring tribe:

Toshi heard an audible voice directing him to go to the land of the Lothas so he requested an elder, Mr. Imdong to accompany him but [Imdong] was reluctant to accompany him as it was time for clearing the weeds in his field. So in order to comply with God's revelation-direction, they went to the field and commanded the weeds to stop growing, then they went to Phiro and Shaki villages and a great revival broke out there.[48]

So the elder, almost as if making a bargain with our Lord, only went with the evangelist when he had used the Lord's authority to help with his normal farming work—to stop the weeds from growing in his fields. It's fortunate he went, as he would be part of one of the most amazing manifestations of the first wave of the Holy Spirit. Mhono remembers hearing about this as a young girl—imagine growing up with this kind of report circulating around you:

> When [revival] people were praying in the church, the villagers saw the church building being raised up towards heaven on the morning of April 18, 1954. It was a time for the villagers to go to the fields and as such all the villagers witnessed it. The villagers pleaded for mercy because they thought the villagers who were praying in the church were being taken to heaven leaving them behind. The church building came back down and settled on the ground.

To the amazement of the villagers, the building landed two inches off from its original position—so the miracle couldn't be denied. "Seeing that, the whole village came to the Lord." The account concludes with the personal detail about the elder's farm work: "After a month, evangelist I. Toshi and Mr. Imdong both returned and saw that God stopped the weeds," but that the rice and other crops had grown well.[49]

This isn't the only instance of the Lord's move affecting agricultural cultivation. Even today in the Peren district of the Zeliangrong tribe, the interviewers have personally tasted cucumbers sweeter and better than those raised elsewhere in India, and the explanation is: a fruit of revival! Mhono Murry was asked whether there were nightly meetings during the revival time in Okotso and agricultural cultivation came up in her account. She told how the Okotso village people ended up doing what the Ao villagers they had "spied" on did: "They didn't go to fields; they prayed and prayed and prayed, while praying many people went [out] in the Spirit." After people would come back from being out in the Spirit, they would tell about visits to heaven or other heavenly things, and those listening were entranced. But, Mhono said, the people opposed to the revival would say scornfully, "Let's see what they will eat! Let's see next year what they will eat. They will come to us begging." Then harvesttime came, and those involved in the revival got more than the other people who were going to fields every day! Mhono said "It went on like that for several years."

Ponder and Apply

Believers have understood our human role in responding to our Lord's initiative in different ways since Jesus walked among us. There have been different understandings on the most basic of responses: How is one saved? Even today there are some who believe in Jesus but aren't certain they will be with Him when they die. Yet even a superficial reading of 1 John highlights God's intent that His people can be assured they are safe with Him. God wants us to know we have passed from death to life.

As we start living out a friendship with Him, the relationship develops and we move beyond simple propositions and statements about His love, to living in it. Our focus is refined and our trust grows. As believers, we're "entitled" to things, to benefits—and yet, we're also completely aware that any things or benefits are entirely His to bestow. So our human framework of "demanding our rights" doesn't seem appropriate—and usually doesn't bring the results we want anyway!

One place to start pondering our own role in starting revival is John 10:27: "My sheep hear my voice, and I know them, and they follow me." This is because faith—our trust in God—comes as we *hear* His word to us—his *rhema,* living, active, compelling word. Not just a general exhortation or promise on a page of a printed Bible—but His word directly to our hearts! "Faith comes from hearing, and hearing through the word of Christ" (Romans 10:17).[50]

As we obey what have we heard Him say to us, no doubt we'll hear more. Our role in starting revival is to listen—and obey! Tied to this is the promise that our hunger will be rewarded:

Ask, and it will be given to you; seek, and you will find; knock, and it will be opened to you. For everyone who asks receives, and the one who seeks finds, and to the one who knocks it will be opened. (*Matthew 7:7–8*)

What have you heard today? Have you obeyed?

CHAPTER 7·

The Fruits of Revival Are Personal

The fruit of the Spirit is love, joy, peace, patience, kindness, goodness, faithfulness, gentleness, self-control. (*Galatians 5:22–23*)

"During these revival days, I was touched by the fire of the Holy Spirit and was very happy as a young man. I thought this joy would last all my days; but I soon came short of His glory, due to a lack of spiritual guidance and feeding."[51] Uncle Murry wrote these words in 1991 as he looked back on the 1950s. His words show his high standards but reflect something else as well—a lack of leaders and shepherds. One of his sons-in-law remembers Uncle Murry describing the '50s revival as his "born again" time. We'll see in chapter 10, "High Tide of the Spirit," that his baptism in the Spirit only came in 1977, more than two decades later. Now getting lifted into the air by the Spirit, or even simply being "touched by the fire of the Holy Spirit" would seem to qualify as being "immersed" or "baptized" in the Spirit. But since I was knocked down by the Spirit several months before being released in the gift of tongues and being assured of the Spirit's indwelling presence in my life, I can appreciate that Uncle Murry didn't see his initial experience as his Holy Spirit baptism.

Still, the fruit of the Spirit showed up in a big way. Uncle Murry's heart was so filled with the love of God he could surmount a major test two years afterward, during his studies for his college exams. A fellow student became envious of his academic achievements and attempted to knife him to death. Fortunately, the student's surprise stab missed and Yaniethung was able to escape and eventually find refuge in a teacher's lodging. When the two students were called before the school authorities to find out what happened, Yaniethung started off by saying: "I forgive him in the name of Jesus."[52] This open and forgiving attitude of heart would serve Yaniethung well throughout his life, as he would be betrayed and wronged during his government service and in his ministry work.

Meanwhile, his future father-in-law Merithung was growing in his faith. His memoir booklet describes an experience in 1957 at the house of the Baptist pastor of Wokha, the nearest large town to the village of Okotso. Merithung said that as he listened to a visiting preacher, "the word of God completely caught my attention. As I listened the word of God flowed into my inner man and tasted as sweet as honey in my physical mouth." Then Merithung started sweating profusely to the point that it was noticeable, and this greatly embarrassed him. In fact, he was so embarrassed that when the same preacher came to Merithung's house later in the day Merithung didn't want to let him in the door. Still, Merithung had to receive him— and the preacher proceeded to encourage him with the word of God. Then a group of family and neighbors gathered for prayer like Merithung "had never experienced before. The words of my prayer to God flowed so spontaneously that I could not stop although others had finished their prayers. My prayer became sweeter and sweeter" to the point that Merithung "was transported in the Spirit to somewhere in heaven and began to pray in some unknown tongue: After the prayer I was wonderstruck and speechless at my own strange experience." Merithung remembered that after this experience the preacher related that he'd seen a flame of fire come down and rest on Merithung's head.

Later that same year, he left a public holiday celebration because of a strong urge to go home and pray.

As the urge, like a voice from my heart, became stronger, I slipped away from the crowd and went home. After a few minutes of praying, sitting on my bed, I heard a loud clear voice from heaven which said in English, "Advice is in Romans." As I heard the voice, my heart seemed to leap upward, but I did not feel pain. Then I began to pray "Lord Jesus, if the matter is so, I will go through the book of Romans and I will not sleep on my bed or take food until the truth is revealed to me." Therefore from noon until evening I read the book of Romans verse by verse lingering carefully on various passages to discern the truth and I reached chapter 6 and was deeply touched by verses 17 and 18 which reads thus, "But God be thanked that ye were servants of sin but ye have obeyed from the heart that form of doctrine which was delivered you. Being then made free from sin, ye became servants of righteousness." As the inner meaning of the passage unfolded before me, my heart melted at the grace of God. Weeping and shedding tears of joy and thanksgiving I earnestly began to pray. As I was praying, I was lifted by the Holy Spirit somewhere in paradise and in my vision I saw an angel standing at the door of heaven holding a bowl filled with burning charcoal, and a huge dog which was approaching me. The angel threw the charcoal and as it rained down on the dog, it disappeared. Then immediately Jesus appeared and I prayed under His feet in an unknown tongue as the Spirit gave me utterance. He said to me, "Henceforth commit no more sin," and he departed from me.

Then I proceeded my pilgrimage farther and I found myself standing at a beautiful breezy land where I heard deep voices of a multitude of people on the right hand saying, "Set free! Set free! Set free," and on the left I heard another multitude of mixed people shouting the same message in what I learned to be Greek and

Hindi. I did not see the multitudes but heard their voices only. I woke up from this great trance singing a new song which I have now forgotten. But I hope to sing it when the kingdom of God comes. This was the first appearance of Jesus Christ to me.[53]

The supernatural evidence of God wasn't confined to Okotso and Wokha but showed up in different ways during the 1950s. After detailing how believers in another Lotha village, Mungya, were harassed for following the revival, the Nagaland Christian Revival Church history records what happened next:

On 30th Oct. 1957, the believers were having a whole night prayer behind closed doors. At about midnight, every other person in the village was lifted up from their bed and thrown on the floor. There was no earthquake but it was a miracle. The villagers rushed to the church and knocked at the doors and windows to let them join the prayer meeting. A great revival broke out. That night, everyone who came for the prayer meeting were baptized in the Holy Spirit with the evidence of speaking in tongues.

But that wasn't the only remarkable indication of God's presence Mungya believers received. The history goes on to detail that "as the Israelites were provided manna, Mungya believers were provided mushrooms in a miraculous way." In that area there's a wild mushroom that's quite a delicacy, and rare enough that only a few people will get a handful at most during its normal growing season. But for three years "that mushroom sprouted in abundance all around the village." Everybody could collect basketfuls, and people collected it every day[54] for the entire month and a half of its growing season during May and June. This miraculous supply of food hadn't happened before, and hasn't since that revival season.

So in that revival atmosphere, Merithung was struggling with a big decision: Should he leave his secure government job, which was at least providing for his family, and launch out as an itinerant preacher with no assured income? As we'll see in the next chapter, his daughter Mhono viewed his decision as being made as abruptly as the way he left school in Shillong: *His brother had died, and Merithung quit school, burned all his books, and went back to his village.* "Why should I study? My brother just died and I'm here?"[55] He'd been enough years in Shillong to learn "British English," as his World War II experience showed, but he had no interest in staying on when there appeared to be no purpose to it.

But Merithung's own words say he thought long and hard about this decision. He was about 45 years of age now, a man with a large family of eight children.

> One noon time in April 1958, I was praying under a chestnut tree near my house. . . . I was struggling to make a decision about God's repeated call to His service. In my prayer I grumbled saying "Lord Jesus you know that I am as poor as a church mouse. If I leave my job, how will I look after my family?" Immediately after I concluded my prayer, I heard an audible voice from heaven which said, "If you worry for yourself what is there for Me to worry for you? God's blessings do not come in luxurious abundance: it is provided according to need. The remaining portion remains hidden, and by faith you will receive it whenever need arises."
>
> I was very much amazed at this message and meditated on it for several days before telling it to my dear wife. At last I very carefully disclosed this message to my dear wife and she was excited and kept herself quiet without a word for a good number of days. Afterward, she said to me, "If it's God's will we must obey Him and you better go. I will try my best to look after the children." Thus with my wife's consent I resigned from Government service and became a full-time servant of the Lord.[56]

With such steps of obedience, a visitation of God is sustained. Let's note that part of the mystery of supernatural occurrences is their definition and timing—while they're happening, it may not be clear to many people that a season has started. Looking across the entire "field" of the Naga people, we can see that some people, some villages, might have been touched between 1952–1954, and others between 1957–60—and that there were still significant supernatural events going on in the 1960s among a remnant.

Ponder and Apply

Although it's not as dramatic or as easily described as supernatural events, our interviews with this Naga family left us impressed at the depth of the love of Christ and human compassion and forgiveness they could walk in. Do we?

Peter Kreeft's adaptation of Augustine of Hippo's words: "My love is my destiny, my gravity, my *gravitas,* my weight, my fate"[57] is a great way of saying that love is what it's all about.

CHAPTER 8

Families Pay a Price for Revival

And Jesus said to him, "Foxes have holes, and birds of the air have nests, but the Son of Man has nowhere to lay his head." (*Matthew 8:20*)

Then He [Jesus] went home, and the crowd gathered again, so that they could not even eat. And when his family heard it, they went out to seize him, for they were saying, "He is out of his mind." (*Mark 3:20–21*)

Mhono remembers her father's launch into ministry from a different perspective than her father's account, more like the way he left school: "Abruptly my father resigned from his government job —he was getting a little bit of pay and with that maintaining the family—but when God called him, he did not think anything about the maintenance of the family. He just resigned!" She said that after this Merithung took his Bible and went out, going from village to village, preaching the word of God. The way she remembered it, her mother's agreement to the call to ministry came *after* the start of Merithung's ministry work, and that at first, "My mother felt really sad. 'How can I feed so many children?' But my father didn't worry at all." She said her father's attitude was simply, "God will take care of it." But Merithung's account and Mhono's end up at the same place: "But at last, my mother agreed with Papa, and she took the responsibility of taking care of her children."

Mhono then described how the family then lived with so little, as all the children helped out once their school day was over:

> Mother assigned us each work. We go to clean the garden. . . . We go to clean the paddy field. We go to collect food for pigs. We go to collect firewood. At that time there was no water supply—we went to the river for washing clothes. . . . Then we bound rice with our hand. . . . And when we get holiday Mother used to take us to earn money.

So how did they earn money on a holiday? At that point in their area of Nagaland, there was no ready supply of sand for the concrete which is critical for building construction there. So the children would collect soft stones, their mother would beat the stones with a metal rod, and then the children would sift the results. A day's work might be ten or fifteen siftings, which could be sold for five to ten rupees. That would allow their mother to buy two pounds of meat, which among the nine mouths might only amount to two bites apiece—and that was their holiday treat!

Merithung describes his own work during this time:

> Meanwhile I continued to preach the Gospel as a free preacher visiting various villages. In the month of October 1959, a revival meeting was held at Lungtsung Baptist church with 24 elders—husbands and wives, confessing our sins. As I was praying kneeling down on the pulpit, I was transported to another world—whether in the body or out of the body I do not know; only God knows. There I saw the Lord Jesus in a crystal garment standing over my

head and looking upon me steadfastly. Then rain like rain on a sunny spring day showered on me.

Sometimes the indication of a visitation of God is simply an "uptick" in the level of what could be considered normal spiritual work in a given body or church. For instance, Merithung went on to recall what happened later that day after his vision of Jesus:

> In the evening of the same day another prayer meeting with the 24 elders continued till midnight. While we were praying, in a vision, I saw a beautiful white bird advancing steadily towards us, and when it reached the church building an elephant Satan[58] rushed out of the church [building] through the main door. As we continued praying two men and one woman were baptized in the Holy Spirit. The woman is still serving the Lord with the gift of prophecy.[59]

Merithung did have regular pay for a time in his gospel service, as in January 1959 he went to the Lotha Baptist Mission center at Vankhosung "to work as a Bible translator on a monthly salary of 150 rupees." Sadly this support only lasted thirteen months, because of the division of beliefs which emerged after the visitation of the Holy Spirit. In Merithung's own words after mentioning but not describing the differences over doctrine: "I was expelled from the Mission Center in February 1962."[60] Although Merithung doesn't specify, no doubt the key difference was over the doctrine of the present-day work of Holy Spirit in believers. Often moves of God do include reports of opponents. Most opponents are no doubt well-meaning, but in their concern to protect "truth" they end up missing and even hindering everyone's experience of "The Truth"—the person of Jesus. Certainly this happened here.

Merithung remained interested in translating the Bible into the Lotha language, which would bring a different form of trouble later. We'll cover this in chapter 20, "Revival and Division."

Once again without regular wages, the family continued to be in need. Merithung wrote later about one incident which expands on Mhono's memories:

> After visiting various villages in Nagaland with good seeds of the Gospel of Jesus Christ, one day in the month of November 1962 I returned home and found my children in dirty rags having no food at home. However, trusting in the Lord, I determined again to proceed on tour that very morning. After having food,[61] when I was about to step out of the door, I was confronted by a family crisis. My dear wife was sitting gloomily in a corner of the kitchen asking me for 100 rupees to meet the immediate needs of the poor children; *Oh, what to do*, I asked myself and prayed to God who had promised me previously. Then she reduced her demand to only 50 rupees.
>
> Meanwhile, in a vision, I saw a man coming towards my house. Immediately, he stepped in the kitchen where we were mournfully sitting and gave her 50 rupees. It was a miracle![62]

He also recounted how almost precisely the same incident occurred five months later, in March 1963, even down to the detail of his wife asking for 100 rupees and then reducing her request to 50. But this time it was a lady believer who came and gave the money to Merithung![63] How he was able to travel with no funds, he doesn't explain! And soon there were only seven children at home as his eldest daughter Mhono would be married in December of 1963 after completing her Grade 10 exams. The arrangement had been made several years earlier, when Mhono was age 14. L. Yaniethung Murry came to their home in Wokha to ask Merithung for her hand, as culturally the father was the one who arranged his daughters' marriages. The age gap between Yaniethung and Mhono was nothing unusual in the culture. Asked how or where Yaniethung had seen her, Mhono wasn't sure:

> I don't know where he saw me. I don't know. We didn't share so much. When we were young, our headmaster, who was a good

Christian, he made us sing so many songs for the church service, because he taught us songs. Maybe in that kind of activity he might have seen me. When I was a young girl, I was SOOOO shy. SOOO shy—I did not say a word in front of people. I could not.

Merithung was willing to be guided by Holy Spirit. Mhono remembers what happened:

My poppa was very much doubtful whether to accept him, or not. Then he went down to one village for revival campaign, to Changsu. There one woman was prophesying in the village. At that time, nobody knew. The lady prophesied, "Oh God is telling Merithung—my father's name is Merithung—to take care of Yani-ethung." So my father was very much surprised! Oh, maybe it's the will of God! Then only he accepted. At that time I was quite young; I did not know anything [about the marriage arrangement]!

Some four years later, on December 18, 1963, the couple were married. Mhono saw her dad and her husband become coworkers for revival. "My father had great hope, had great confidence in him. He loved him so much! He loved him so much!" Merithung's impulsive nature and generosity showed through: "He tried to give us his house. But I objected—because of my brothers, my sisters, so many brothers, so many sisters, eight of us, so how can we take this?"

Ponder and Apply

As we look at Merithung's extraordinary sacrifice—and the sacrifice of his family—it's well to ponder: Have we been asked to take a step or give up something? Where we've answered that call, let's celebrate and continue to trust there will be lasting fruit—and if we have yet to obey, seek our Lord to see if there's still time or whether the opportunity has passed. If the opportunity has passed, repent and obey next time.

Although the focus in Mhono's remembrances was on the financial hardship and the social shame the family lived through, time together may have been another sacrifice. Rocky Gram describes a season during the move of God in Argentina which no doubt paralleled Merithung's schedule, as pastors would

> night after night hold services and then pray for the sick and needy until after midnight. The normal time for eating supper for many of them has become one thirty or two o'clock in the morning. A few days ago I called a pastor, and his wife mentioned that he wasn't in. As I commented on how busy he must be, she said, "Yes, we hardly have any time together. But it is worth it for the fruit of these days. We have to take advantage of them!" . . . In the days when Carlos Annacondia held his first evangelistic campaigns in La Plata, some of the leaders did not even bother to undress when they went to bed. Someone was always coming in the middle of the night, asking for healing or bringing a person who was demon-possessed,[64] and they had to be ready to help. That takes commitment.[65]

What these families in Nagaland encountered of our Lord sustained their commitment, and yet in some way helped sustain the revival through their sacrifice and hunger. Their lives show how dangerous the infection of revival fever or a visitation virus can be. There's always a cross, a point of death, to release love. To be "stronger than death"—to conquer death—there must be a death to self and selfishness.

Their lives embraced, perhaps without knowing it, the paradox that loving God can be bittersweet. "Bitter" because we don't gain or possess that which we long for in fullness—more of our Lord. Yet "sweet" because to long for God, to pursue our Lord, is better than possessing the whole world. It's longing that sustains revival.

> I will seek him whom my soul loves. I sought him, but found him not. (*Song of Songs 3:2*)

CHAPTER 9

Do "a Little Bit Extreme" Remnants Sustain Revival?

But others said, "How can a man who is a sinner do such signs?" And there was division among them. (*John 9:16b*)

The division following supernatural moves of God is certainly consistent with what happened during Jesus's earthly ministry. Human hearts respond to the Spirit's work, and that involves individual and group choices. Therefore, the fruit is different from one to another. In nature, even the fruit growing from the same root system on an apple tree will be different—one apple gets attacked by a worm, another has more sun. Still, we can wonder how Jesus's prayer that we as believers will be one is going to be worked out if it's not shown when His kingship is most visible during a visitation of God. We can ponder how apparently equally sincere and devout hearts can end up at odds—and how it fits with the ongoing drama of God working out His purposes on the planet.

The uneven distribution of the 1950s revival shows in a brief historical summary given in the Nagaland Christian Revival Church's fifty-year-jubilee booklet. The booklet gives as examples three villages that were touched: Chedema, Menguzuma, and Longkhüm (where the leaders highlighted were Rikum and Toshi, mentioned earlier).[66] The booklet also adds: "Revival did occur in many places but did not spread beyond the respective church or locality." It briefly paints a glowing picture of what did happen where people were touched:

> They were singing and praying all over the land, even in the jungles and fields. After the day's work they used to gather in houses to worship God for hours together, even throughout the nights, sometimes skipping meals. . . . [W]herever revival spreads the same phenomena occurred. Packets of tobacco and barrels of local wine were thrown away. Touched by the Holy Spirit they went from door to door, asking for forgiveness, crying with loud voices, confessing their sins.[67]

Some specific supernatural interventions are described:

> Mr. Mhonlumo of Tsüngiki village [a village of the Lotha tribe] received the Lord as his personal savior at age 98. He received the Baptism of the Holy Ghost at the age of 102. He was so old that he could not walk but crawl. But miraculously, after he came to the Lord, he could walk without a walking stick. It is said that new hair began to grow on his head though they were gray. It is also said that again his teeth reappeared. He used to say: "Look! Revival teeth, revival hair. Believe Jesus!"[68]

The NCRC history includes some other incidents that happened among the Ao tribe, the neighbors to the Lothas:

> In Mokokchung town some students prayed for kerosene for their lamps for studying (as there was no electricity then). Kerosene miraculously gushed out from the ground just in their compound,

which has never happened before or after, but was just enough for the school examination period.

During Indian Army operation, three old women of Long-khüm village were hiding in a cave in the jungle. There was nobody to bring food for them. When they prayed to God for food a crow used to bring bread (chapati and puri)[69] from the army camp every morning. They were fed like Elijah for three months.

Somewhat like the Hebrews escaping Egyptian slavery, the women grew tired of this daily repetition:

They were fed up with bread and when they prayed for meat a wild cat brought a big wild fowl and left it just at the entrance of the cave for them. Also there was a bee hive nearby on the top of a tree and every morning they found some larvae (a delicacy) fallen on the ground which they collected and enjoyed.[70]

After telling one instance of a speaker switching over to preach in a language he didn't know, the history relates another instance that involves the family we're following:

Evangelist I. Toshi was preaching in English and Merithung was interpreting into Lotha dialect. The audience heard both of them speaking in Lotha. The people were wondering why interpretation was needed when both of them were preaching in the Lotha dialect. But the speaker did not know even a word of the Lotha dialect.[71]

The history notes: "These were the signs to unbelievers as on the day of Pentecost in Jerusalem." This incident supports the view that listeners were given a gift of "hearing in tongues" on the day of Pentecost, as contrasted with the view that there were a dozen different preachers at Pentecost, speaking a dozen different languages, with the hearers conveniently matched up with the speakers.[72] The account also shows the incredible challenges involved in communicating the gospel among the different tribes—Merithung's aptitude with English, which was serving as a bridge language like Greek in the time of Christ, was proving important.[73] Perhaps part of the reason the different local visitations didn't spread as widely in the 1950s as they would in the 1970s was language barriers. This wasn't Wales or the Hebrides, where all inhabitants could be reached in one or two languages.

The family we're following shows up later on as well in the NCRC history:

> Back in Wokha, a revival meeting was held. Altogether 17 believers took baptism for the first time on Sept. 17, 1957. After water baptism, when they prayed, the Holy Spirit fell upon them with great power and many believers received baptism in Holy Ghost with the sign of speaking in tongues for the first time in Nagaland.[74] Many young people committed their lives to serve the Lord. Some of them even left educational institutions, various professions and jobs. Among those, a prominent leader, Rev. E. Merithung Mozhüi resigned from a lucrative government job, and started preaching. He was the first General Secretary of NCRC.[75]

After these extraordinary happenings, this history sadly has to move on to cover the division among Nagas during the 1960s on the issue of revival:

> The then Church leaders, misunderstood the revival movement and they labeled the work of the Holy Spirit as a heresy and the spiritual experiences as fanaticism. The opposition was followed by severe persecutions from the people. The revival preachers were not allowed to preach and wherever they went various hindrances were preplanned to reject and persecute them. In a particular incident, before the preachers reached the place, a letter was already

dispatched in advance indicating the preachers deserved the death sentence. This letter was revealed to the preachers, when the people were touched by the Holy Spirit and experienced wondrous works of God.[76]

Here's another instance showing how deep the division was in those days:

> In 1965 Sastami Church building was destroyed four times and the building materials were confiscated by those who opposed the revival movement. Four granaries full of paddy [rice] belonging to the church were also taken away. The church elders were forced to do tough manual work as they refused to deny the works of the Holy Spirit in their lives. Twelve church elders were taken into prison for forty days with extensive labor and scarce food. They were taken for trial to be condemned and sentenced for further hardship and imprisonment.

Fortunately, there appears to have been some divine intervention for these elders, bearing witness to the work of the Spirit. At their first hearing, the judge started feeling sick and ended up vomiting "a lot." So "the trial was delayed." When they were to appear next, a fire broke out nearby ("from nowhere" the account notes) and gutted a few homes, so again their hearing was postponed. Finally, after forty days the elders were sent back home, with a warning that they should quit their revival practices of prayer, mass praise, and worship, and not share testimonies or speak in tongues.[77] One is reminded of the Sanhedrin's words to Peter and John not to speak in the name of Jesus (Acts 4:18; 5:40). The booklet sums up the intense division: "Indeed, some preachers lost their lives through false instigations and reports in the midst of political turmoil,[78] although many were miraculously saved. The revival people were excommunicated from the churches. They were prohibited from preaching, giving testimony and praying."[79]

What was the division over? The NCRC booklet details these specific doctrinal disagreements:

1. Assurance of salvation here on earth is not possible. So revival believers giving testimony of personal salvation experience is unacceptable.

2. Except on the set days and timings made by the church, it is fanatical to pray, sing, worship and preach. Worshiping and preaching on other days are not allowed. Any violation of these is subject to punishment.

3. Worship and prayer should be with all reverence, solemnity and calm. A priestly prayer is considered enough. Mass prayer with shouting, crying and undisciplined physical movements like jumping, waving and clapping hands should not be allowed.

4. Revival is a new religion. So every faithful church member should oppose it.

5. The so-called receiving of the "Baptism in the Holy Ghost" is a heresy because the Holy Spirit is already given to us and the days of such experiences as claimed by the revivalists are over. The days of the Holy Spirit working are past and not for us.

6. Divine gifts, healings, speaking in tongues, visions, prophecies and such like as claimed by the revivalists as spiritual gifts are all false. Such divinations are devilish.

7. Without having a theological background or a degree, one is neither entitled or qualified to preach or teach. So ignorant and naïve revival preachers should not be allowed to preach the Gospel.[80]

This is the "revivalist" explanation of the differences which led to a remnant of believers starting new churches. The account goes on to say the birth of the new denomination wasn't simply a reaction to people being rejected or persecuted for their experiences, but due to people searching for a new expression of what they'd experienced in the Lord. Most notably, particularly given both Merithung and Uncle Murry's experiences of being water-baptized without believing, the NCRC history notes that the revivalists practiced water baptism only after a person had repented and believed: "They understood that water baptism without repentance was of no use. This was outrageously opposed by the church leaders." In addition, speaking in tongues and the operation of the gifts of the Holy Spirit couldn't be expressed in the existing church structure. When believers were living in the reality of these experiences, "they needed teachings and guidance which the existing church could neither tolerate or accommodate." So a new network of revival churches came into being in Nagaland, recognizing the reality of people's experience and the need to uphold this reality from the Bible.[81]

The intense division did affect Merithung—his expulsion from the Bible translation work in 1962 was effectively an excommunication! Mhono remembered another incident among the Lotha people from 1960, showing the opposition to anything outside of the normal schedule of church activities. An old man whose hair was completely white had fallen deeply in love with Jesus "SOOOO much." He would get up at 3:30 or 4:00 a.m.[82] and climb up the hill to what was then the small church building in Wokha.

> He used to pray inside the church, for the whole Lotha people. Then the church leaders were not happy—they were not happy. So they locked the church door because this old man used to go inside and pray. Then when he went up to the church and saw the door locked, he stood there and shouted "Hallelujah! Praise the Lord!" and the lock opened. Like that, the lock opened itself.

Asked about how those who believed in revival and who'd been cast adrift from the established churches were cared for, Mhono said, "Pastoral care? There was no pastoral care." As she saw it, at that time all the churches were under the control of the Baptist mission center (although by this time the missionaries had been gone for several years) and "they were not interested." So as those who'd experienced revival met in separate prayer meetings or worship times, "anyone who is a little matured in the faith, they cared for the group." But the lack of support did contribute to some backsliding, or going back to the existing church structure. In Mhono's words, "the very few remnant became a different group. They became separated from the main denominational stream." She added something a moment later about why those who became the remnant were willing to be:

> When revival comes, healing is a common experience. Anyone who's old and sickly, if he or she accepts revival, they become young again. Very strong, healthy, like that. So those people who experienced that, that kind of life, they—they cannot deny it! So even though there is persecution or there is some criticism or hatred, they still trust.

Later in that talk she expanded on the situation in the '60s, saying there were so few leaders working with her father, and so he found himself taking the lead:

> *Interviewer:* You're still at home, your mom has all eight children, and your dad is taking charge of revival meetings?
>
> *Mhono:* Yeah, he goes around to villages. Everybody used to say, "Merithung's group, Merithung's group," like that. All of them go to my father for preaching.
>
> *Interviewer:* As a child, what were you thinking?
>
> *Mhono:* At that time *(laughs)*, I was a teenager, maybe 13, 14, like that. So at that time, we did not know anything, and we had . . . so much shame. . . . We were ashamed to go to school. . . . It was a TOUGH time for us. Because ALL our friends belonged to another group. Because here the culture is so different, no? Feeling shy, feeling shame, it is the main thing.

She described how she didn't know how to assert herself, and would be so defeated around her peers from the established church: "We couldn't stand for our rights . . . always feeling shame." Asked if she went on any of her father's preaching trips, she brightened up:

> When there is a revival convention, we were happy to go. Because there so many people came. We did not feel shy anymore, but when we came back to our opponents' area, we would not be so brave. I should not say "opponents" but when we come to worship time then automatically there comes division. Your group—our group—like that. It was in the mental attitude of the people. So even though they did not speak anything immediately that kind of feeling came. So we would not be so brave then.

Another time Mhono shed more light on what it was like to be in a revival leader's family:

> So if my mother hadn't had big faith, she would not be able to do it, because my father was also a little bit—what should I say? A little bit extreme. Whatever he wanted to do—first of all, he would pray and ask God, and if he gets green signal from God, then he would just do it! My father was that kind of man. So any woman, any ordinary woman, would find it difficult to cope with him.

Mhono went right on sharing in this reflective mood, evaluating the cost on the family of her father's zeal and impulsive obedience, and her mother's acquiescence: "Now when they are gone we remember what they taught us, what they did for the people, for the society and for the children." And she sees some of their work was good, and some of it wasn't so good, "because man is not perfect." Even a visitation of God doesn't change that reality.

Because of the conflict, people who viewed themselves as revivalists began banding together in the early 1960s. Merithung's brief memoir includes this account of those days. It may be significant he starts with the third-person pronoun and then switches to second-person:

> After a few years of rejoicing under the guidance of the Holy Spirit, they organized a revival convention which took place in Keruma Basa from February 1–4, 1961. In this revival convention about 600 believers gathered together and were encircled by Indian army personnel. In such danger . . . we cried to God for mercy and heaven came down and glory filled our souls, which caused us to sing the song "Heaven came down and glory filled my soul."[83]

Merithung doesn't explain how the believers were delivered, but the NCRC history booklet does:

> God Himself taught the power of praise and worship in this convention. A prohibitory order was imposed by the government all over Nagaland . . . which banned more than four people gathering at a time and to shoot at sight all violators. . . . (Keruma village was a staunch supporter of the Naga National Movement. They held meetings with many renowned underground leaders. The villagers even confronted the Indian Army by trying to obstruct their entry into the village. The Army targeted the village as a Naga Nationalist center.) During the convention, they surrounded the congregation and they were sure to be fired upon or tortured. At that moment a prophecy was uttered to shout "Praise the Lord" (in English) after every prayer or testimony. Many of the simple illiterate villagers did not understand the meaning but as per the direction of the Holy Spirit they shouted it at the top of their voice. Hearing that the army captain[84] understood the gathering to be a religious one and refrained from taking any action against them. After the convention, on their way back home, when the believers were confronted by Indian soldiers they raised both arms and shouted "Praise the Lord" and they were left alone without any harm. Later on it was

learnt through a reliable source that the Army had issued a circular stating that those people saying "Praise the Lord" should not be harmed. It was a password given by the Lord.[85]

This account follows the history telling how the convention was organized and selected several officers, including Merithung Mozhüi as general secretary. Merithung continues his history:

The second revival convention was held Jan. 6–9, 1962 in the village of Gariphema. During this convention many elderly people who had been cast out from their churches came with heavy hearts and in dilemma whether to go forward or to go back and in course of discussion and prayer a portion of scripture at Acts 11:26 was revealed to an elderly pastor—Antioch Christian Church.

But in a short course of time it was revealed that there are many Christian Churches in the world. But this newly born Christian Church was distinguished by inserting "Revival" in between the two C's.[86]

And thus was born another denomination: Christian Revival Church. Merithung served as general secretary for the first five years. Then in 1967, at the now annual convention, the NCRC[87] records that he was elected president of the new denomination, as his predecessor was going abroad for studies. Merithung served in that role about three years until his predecessor returned to resume the role.[88] During this fluid time, he was also key in getting the outside Assemblies of God movement connected with the "revivalists." The Assemblies of God–East India history mentions a key meeting in 1964 at his home, with representatives of ten churches among the Lotha tribe. Mark Buntain, an Assemblies of God missionary based in Kolkata, was eventually invited as a speaker for the annual revivalists' convention, which led to some wanting to affiliate with Assemblies of God as an organization. "On February 13, 1972, the 1st

Nagaland (Assemblies of God) District Conference was convened at Mungya village and the elected office bearers were . . . Rev. E. M. Mozhüi, District Secretary."[89] (Remember, Mungya was a village powerfully touched by the Lord in the 1950s wave of the Spirit.) Thus Merithung has the distinction of being a leader in two different denominational groupings—an interesting fulfillment of his dream calling him to serve the Lotha Association.

During the 1960s, Mhono remembers the division between believers, and yet she also remembers love overflowing. She told how in Angami village, an old widow had a banana tree in her field. When the time to harvest bananas came, the widow went and looked up in the tree and discovered someone had already taken her bananas! She was disturbed almost beyond belief, and so sad that someone had stolen from her. She thought and thought about it, and finally decided what to do: "So at nighttime, after everyone was settled in their homes, and about to go to bed . . . she went outside, and shouted to the village people: 'Hear my words—village people! Anyone who cut and took my bananas from my field, ohhh may God bless him!' Really—she shouted like that. 'I forgive him! May God bless him.'" After shouting that at the top of her voice, then the widow was satisfied and at peace. "Brotherly love was so strong at that time" during the 1960s, Mhono concluded.

When Mhono remembered the good her father had done, she specifically listed "the children"—not referring to her own family but others her father had assisted. For some time in the 1960s, he managed an orphanage supported by an American healing evangelist, David Nunn. "My father opened a primary school in the orphanage. So the children were given free education, the children were given clothing, nice bedding, dressed and supplied food."

Sadly, opposition arose here as well. Mhono said this was due to simple envy, and didn't mention any other cause such as doctrinal disputes. After Merithung withdrew and another manager took over, the quality of care went down. It's unclear if the poor management was what caused Nunn to halt his support or if he was simply focusing on another priority, since he funded the start of Kohima Bible College in 1970.[90] But the orphanage did close. Mhono sadly told how grown men who'd been children in the orphanage had come to her and said they could have become "something" if her father had stayed on, but now they "were living a very hard life." As Mhono thought about what happened at the orphanage, she focused on the sin of envy around her: "If anyone sees someone doing good and prospering, they try to pull them down. The society is like this. This world is Satan-infested." Within a few years of the orphanage closing, Merithung would start his own school and bless a generation of children in a different way—more on this in chapter 19, "How Does Abundant Life Work?"

Ponder and Apply

"What are you doing here, Elijah?" He said, "I have been very jealous for the Lord, the God of hosts. For the people of Israel have forsaken Your covenant, thrown down Your altars, and killed Your prophets with the sword, and I, even I only, am left, and they seek my life, to take it away." And the Lord said to him . . . "Yet I will leave seven thousand in Israel, all the knees that have not bowed to Baal, and every mouth that has not kissed him." (*1 Kings 19: 13–15, 18*)

God's words to Elijah remind us there can be a temptation to think we're all alone, that we're a beleaguered remnant—when really we aren't! The teaching and interest in the supernatural work of God in Nagaland waned in the 1960s, to the point other histories barely mention anything happening in the decade. But there were people, even groups of people, that sustained their interest and desire for God to show Himself in mighty works. And they would see amazing things in the mid-'70s.

Of course the fact that the next wave would flow far beyond their ranks and denominational groups is consistent with the wave of the Spirit in the 1950s, flowing outside the Ao tribe to other tribes that hadn't really been involved or aware of God's work.

This pattern of prayer in one place and an outbreak nearby is similar to that in previous revivals. For instance, there was a local outpouring at the beginning of this century in Shelbyville, Tennessee. In January of 2000, Pastor Bryan Nerren led his church on a forty-day fast for revival. They didn't see any particular manifestations or fruit—and then that spring, a series of meetings started at the First Baptist Church of Shelbyville that saw 1,200 people saved in the space of six months (in a county with a population of 38,000). Nerren and his church eventually threw themselves into it—wisely recognizing that "this was that"—that this is what they had prayed for, even if it wasn't in their building.[91]

Certainly I've prayed that wherever I am would be the center of God's visitation—but is it possible that's one of the tests of our hearts? Are we so hungry that we don't care where or through who—that we're simply eager that our Lord reveals more of His glory?

CHAPTER 10

High Tide of the Spirit

When all the people of Israel saw the fire come down and the glory of the Lord on the temple, they bowed down with their faces to the ground on the pavement and worshiped and gave thanks to the Lord, saying, "For He is good, for His steadfast love endures forever." (*2 Chronicles 7:4*)

Uncle Murry saw his personal revival this way:

In 1973 another touch of the Spirit happened to me and my backslidden spirit awakened and came to life. But I gradually cooled down and drifted into the barren land of sin and shame. A remarkable revival broke out in Nagaland in 1977. During this revival on Oct. 19, 1977, I experienced the full anointing of the Holy Spirit, which is the baptism of the Holy Spirit, in my life.[92]

What happened to bring this wave of revival? The degree of human effort and planning leading up to this move of God will challenge those who see the timing of a visitation as strictly a matter of God's sovereign decision. The view which eliminates any human involvement in the timing of visitation generally results in the bad spiritual fruit of disengaging from God, at least at some level. *We need to seek our Lord when He wants to be sought.* (This topic is explored more fully in chapter 14, "How Does Revival Start? (Part II).") In Mhono's view there was human hunger and prayer, which contributed to this third wave of Holy Spirit:

> First wave—people did not organize. Second wave also people did not organize.[93] And third wave though—that also—it's God's timing. Yeah, third wave—people might have prayed sooooo much because first wave died down, second wave died down. Now there were some remnants, and those remnants must have prayed for the third wave of revival. Now, this third wave of revival broke out in Ao area, Mokokchung area.

So what was involved in people seeking this wave of revival? We'll quote at length from Akümla Longkumer's history of the 1970s revival to give the framework for what was surrounding the Murry family's experience. This history focuses on events and steps which can be recounted afterward, so it can almost come across as a business memo![94] Longkumer records that starting in 1967, the Ao Baptist churches focused on one theme each year, leading up to their centennial in 1972 (as the first Ao believers were baptized in 1872).

> In 1971, stressing the theme, "Proclamation of the Gospel," the Ao Baptist churches planned a year-round chain of prayer (January–December 1971). One of the main prayer items was for revival in the Church . . . that there may be a world-wide revival of the Spirit and that the revival may begin in Nagaland.[95]

She goes on to mention the visit of Stanley Mooneyham with a World Vision team to Nagaland and the Graham meetings in Kohima as stirring interest in revival. "Attendance at the Graham meetings approximated 100,000 and gave Christian Nagas a great boost in morale."[96] In fact, there was evidently intense human interaction to bring about Graham's visit. In his ministry report, filmed on location for the ministry's supporters, Graham said:

> In all my years of ministry I've never been under such pressure[97] from a group of God-fearing people as the Naga people to help them come and celebrate the coming of Christianity to Nagaland by holding a crusade. In spite of the many dangers here and they're very real, we decided to come and encourage these thousands of Christians who love Jesus Christ as Lord and Savior.[98]

He went on to describe the spiritual situation:

> One of the problems of evangelism here in Nagaland is similar to the one we face in America and Europe. There are thousands of people here who profess Christianity as their religion or culture, but have not received Christ as Lord and Savior.[99]

There's also a humorous video clip of Graham speaking to a group of what must be Baptist pastors in the USA where he talks about his trip to Kohima, Nagaland:

> And so when we got there they said their first service was going to be before daylight at 5 in the morning.[100] And they said, "Dr. Graham we're expecting you to teach the word of God at that time." I said, "Well look here," I said, "How about some of my associates taking that?" I said. "I've got two other services tomorrow, one at noon and one in the evening," I said, "I'll take those two. Give that early morning service to one of these others. This fellow here, Charlie Riggs, is one of the greatest Bible teachers in the world!" I said, "How many do you expect?" They said, "We will have at least a hundred thousand." I said, "I'll take that myself!"[101]

The crowd of Baptist pastors laughed appropriately at his self-deprecating humor. Earlier as he'd talked to them, he shared about his trip to Kohima:

I went there for their 100th anniversary of Christianity in Nagaland. And the Baptists had cleared off the roads for us. They had cut down the trees, and they had soldiers behind us with machine guns and soldiers in front with machine guns and uhh (*slight pause*) it was really a Baptist procession! (*Crowd laughter—evidently from Baptist pastors*) From the airport to Kohima—I forgot how many miles it was but they'd had a lot of people killed on that road just in the few weeks before we got there.[102]

Graham also spoke in his ministry film report about the people's hunger:

Here in Kohima, high up in the Himalayas, people are traveling many miles by foot to attend the meetings. Hundreds are praying for new vision, new strength and a renewed faith in their churches. Crowds of many thousands are already attending and many hundreds are coming to know Jesus Christ as Savior and Lord. Hundreds are sleeping out in the open in spite of the cold air.[103]

Mhono Murry saw the Graham meeting as a moment of unity among the believers in 1972, after the separations and divisions starting in the late '50s. Interestingly, her memory includes a disruption, as the independence forces did fire gunshots; she didn't specify where, and didn't know the purpose. Another Naga writer, V. Leno Peseyie-Maase, is a member of the Angami tribe, and wrote a biography of her missionary brother Thino Peseyie. She also mentions a shooting before the Graham meetings:

At this time the North East India regions, and Kohima in particular, were perhaps the most prayed for spots in the world. In spite of the serious situation due to the recent shooting incident on the Kohima to Dimapur road, God in His own time controlled all situations. Many testified that in a most unusual way they were led to experience the truth of the crusade theme which read, "Jesus, the Hope of the World." About 115,000 people heard Dr. Graham's message during the Kohima Crusade. Over 3,250 people made decisions to accept Jesus Christ and many Christians rededicated their lives to God. . . . Following the remarkable Dr. Billy Graham's crusade, a great revival movement broke out throughout Nagaland. As a result a great awakening began in the Angami churches.[104]

While Peseyie-Maase connects the Graham meetings and the revival, there was a gap of some four to five years. In fact, her brother, while attending and being profoundly affected by the Graham meetings, didn't actually get born again until four years later at a gospel camp! As we have said earlier, revival is personal—and God had clearly been at work in her brother's life for years. Before the India Army occupation of Nagaland (so prior to 1955) while he was herding cattle, he was led to go off and pray for two hours on Good Friday afternoon. His fellow cattle-herder teased him, "You seem like you want to become a revivalist."[105] Did his personal revival begin then? Until we see or hear something tangible, it's difficult to say when the work of the Spirit begins.

It is worth noting how impressive the attendance was, given the difficulty of travel within Nagaland. The population of Nagaland in the 1971 census of India was 515,450, so close to one in five residents of Nagaland heard Graham in person. Even allowing for people coming with other motives, the huge attendance shows a deep interest in the things of God.

Let's return to Longkumer's account of the buildup to the revival. The connection with a concern for cross-cultural and world mission is obvious:

Following the Centennial celebrations [and Graham's visit], the Ao Church leaders were confronted with the question, "After Centennial, what?"

One part of the answer was that a "chain of prayer began in 1973 involving all the Ao churches and the neighboring tribal churches."[106] Then Longkumer goes to another part of the answer:

> The answer was a plea to God to 'Make our land a missionary land.'. . . After the Lausanne Congress on World Evangelization (1974) the Naga Church leaders who participated in the Lausanne Congress, called for an All Nagaland Congress on World Evangelization at Dimapur, March 1–9, 1975. Two main subjects were studied during this Conference:
>
> • The History of Revival, Evangelism and Missions.
>
> • The Work of the Holy Spirit in the Church.

The church leaders recognized that to realize this dream of becoming a missionary land, there was a need for revival. All the delegates to the Naga Congress signed a covenant, part of which reads:

> We, the servants of the Lord Jesus Christ in Nagaland determine to carry out the Great Commission of the Lord . . . solemnly dedicate ourselves to launch the following spiritual measures among all Nagaland tribes, beginning from Association Center down to every local church and every home, for the mighty outpouring of the power of the Holy Spirit upon all believers:
>
> 1. To continue organizing prayer cells and Bible study groups involving every home and every Christian.
>
> 2. To continue holding intensive evangelistic crusades in every village and town for revival . . . we therefore resolve to set all Nagaland churches on revival fire beginning in us. God help us!

After the Congress, preparation for revival started in all associational levels. Counsellor trainings, church camps, crusades, Bible studies and prayer cells were conducted. The cry for revival contin- . ued in deep intensity, expectation growing daily.[107]

Longkumer's history continues with the details of the first signs of a supernatural visitation of God:

In July 1975, the Ao Baptist churches conducted a counseling training program for all the Ao church leaders. After the training special prayer and Bible study groups were organized in all local churches. It was during such meetings that the Spirit of God began to move the hearts of the people.

ANAKI: On May 6–9, 1976, the Anaki Baptist Church conducted a special prayer and Bible study which was called the Hour of Revival under the leadership of M. I. Luen who was then an evangelist of Ao Baptist Church Association. On May 8, during a morning prayer meeting, the church members experienced an unusual visitation of the spirit as everyone started crying out aloud confessing their sins. This prayer continued for several hours during which some expressed their joy in laughing out loud while some saw visions of angels appearing in brightness.[108]

This is considered as the beginning of the revival movement although there are some who consider Wameken . . . more phenomenal than Anaki as the beginning. It may be noted here that the pastor of Wameken was one of the Pastors who was present at Anaki revival with other pastors from surrounding churches... What followed after Anaki was a similar repetition of what happened at Anaki although it is true that more phenomenal features accompanied the latter movements.[109]

So what did happen at Wameken that made it "more phenomenal" than Anaki?

Wameken Baptist Church, located in a small village near a big newly established government paper mill, was founded in 1893 by the pioneer American Baptist missionary Dr. Clark. It had been a moderately strong church until 1976, when the incumbent pastor suddenly died. The church at this time was going through spiritual dryness, mainly due to the rise and influence of materialism.

Sensing the spiritual dryness and the need for revival in the church, the church elders, some of whom had been at the Ao Christian Revival Training (1974) with the pastor and also at Counselling Training (1975) decided to call a week of Bible study and prayer for revival. Imdangmeren, the pastor of the Tuli Paper Mill Church who had been at Anaki revival, was invited to lead the Bible study.

Longkumer, quoting another revivalist's account, said the guest pastor started his Bible studies, and the houses were packed for several nights:

> One evening a miracle of healing took place. One old woman by the name of Tsuktishila had a cramped arm, that would not stretch out. As the pastor held her hand and prayed, her hand stretched out and was healed. . . . This miracle had a moving impact upon all those present in the meeting . . . the church members decided to meet in the church hall.[110]

May 28: The meeting began Friday at 8 a.m. Unusual things began to happen. . . .

1. Hearts of people were melted as the word of God was ministered. Unable to hide their sin, people began to make confession of their shortcomings.

2. The Spirit started to work in every individual's heart.

High Tide of the Spirit 101

3. The service lasted for nine hours.

4. The same evening, the meeting began at 7 p.m. and it lasted till 1 a.m. the next morning. However, the people felt no physical thirst and hunger.

5. Individuals stood up to give testimonies of the joy of deliverance from sin through God's forgiving power.

May 29: The meeting began at 8 a.m. and lasted till 11 a.m. The evening service began at 6 p.m. when the Lord visited the youth in a mighty way. The youth who had never prayed, prayed long and loud. The meeting lasted till midnight as young and old people continued to pray and sing together in the Spirit: "God is working . . .".

May 30: It was Sunday and the following things happened:

1. More and more people came to the pulpit to testify.

2. People wept as they prayed.

3. The Holy Spirit continued to touch the people's hearts. Without realizing it, the people stood up in joy saying, "God is working . . ." clapping their hands in spiritual vigor.

4. Those who looked at the revival with a cold attitude in the beginning started to come and began to make confession of sin in deep repentance.

5. There was a special time of prayer of dedication of the Village Administrative Council members during which time all members made confession of their sins.[111]

Before continuing with Longkumer's history, take a moment to imagine local politicians confessing their sins. It's hard to conceive any group more protective of their image, particularly in a culture based on honor and shame. Yet that's what this account of visitations records! The history continues with the next church to be touched:

June 4–6, 1976 the Tuli Town Baptist church conducted its first revival hours. Prior to this the church had already experienced a spiritual renewal during a missionary week program. Toshi Aier, the Pastor of the Tuli Town church, made the following report about the revival in his personal letter dated May 11, 1980:

THE GENERAL FEATURES:

    a. Crying and weeping

    b. Clapping, jumping and singing

    c. Voluntary sharing of personal testimony

    d. Seeing vision of Christ by some individuals

    e. Healing of the sick

    f. Confession of personal sins

    g. Continuation of the service for 10 hours

    h. Conversion of many men of other faith.

CHANGES IN INDIVIDUAL LIFE:

    a. Re-dedication of life

    b. New interest in the study of the Word of God

    c. Enthusiasm in singing, church attendance and preaching

    d. Voluntary giving

CHANGE IN CHURCH LIFE:

    a. Extension of church building

    b. Increase in church income

    c. Regular prayer cells and Bible study

    d. New mission fields in Arunachal and Assam

    e. Creation of a Mission Board.[112]

Longkumer's history goes on to say: "The same year the fire of revival touched almost all the local churches in the Ao area and, by the following year, it spread out throughout the neighboring tribes and to other neighboring tribes . . . in Assam, Manipur and Arunachal Pradesh."[113] So this correlates with Uncle Murry's experience, being part of a neighboring tribe to the Ao, having his personal revival in October 1977. Mhono's personal recollection of these days included a visit to Mokokchung, a key spiritual center for the Ao tribe:

> I went to visit Mokokchung with my sister and as we reached the town we saw the big playground filled with people. And the singers were on one side, the congregation were on the other side. The choir were wearing all white clothes and then they covered their head with white clothes, and then they were leading the congregation in praise and worship. And I was very much touched at that time in Mokokchung town—all the shops selling betelnuts[114]— those shops were closed! There were no shops selling alcohol. There were no shops selling nasty things. It was so cleaned up. That kind of revival. And that revival spread to Lotha area also. And then Sumi area also. Angami area also.

Des Short, president and founder of Faith Bible College, Tauranga, New Zealand, has visited Nagaland seven times. His first visit was in 1990 and he was told about what had happened in the mid-'70s. His first meeting was in Mokokchung. All the leaders he was meeting with had been part of the visitation in the '70s, and they were thrilled to have a guest from the West to share with. Because of the ongoing military conflict, contact with Westerners had been severely restricted by the Indian government, even up to that point. Des remembered his "meals were held in an Army compound, just by the main ground where the revival broke out in 1975. And around the meal table the leaders would share with me what took place when the revival happened." The first story he heard was from the leader at that time:

Before the revival broke out, birds came into the houses of people and even if they were having a meal outside, these little birds would come and sit on the table and then they would speak! . . . They would speak in the dialect of the (person). . . . And the words they spoke were: "Jesus is coming soon!" And so Nagas were hearing this before the revival happened. "Jesus is coming soon. Jesus is coming soon. Jesus is coming soon." And on the day that revival broke out, this man, who was the leader, preached a sermon on Jesus's baptism. And he talked about when Jesus came up out of the water the Holy Spirit in the form of a dove descended upon Him and remained upon Him.

And on this day when he talked about the dove of the Holy Spirit descending upon Jesus, all of a sudden literally thousands and thousands of beautiful doves flew over the congregation of people and hovered there. And he was telling me, and all the other pastors and their wives that were there were nodding their heads and saying "Brother Short, it's true," "Brother Short, it's true—we were there." And I was getting goosebumps all over my body. And then he told me—there's never been any doves in Nagaland—until that particular time. And he preached for 40 minutes and when he said "Amen" at the end of 40 minutes the doves flew away. And a few years had gone by since then—because I was there in 1990. This was 1975. There's never been doves in Nagaland before, and he said there's never been doves since! So it was just God confirming the word with signs and wonders following. And with what happened on that day, word got out so quickly.

Des said the crowd grew much bigger in the evening:

It was full moon that night. The ground got lit up with the brilliancy of the moon—they had primitive lighting out for the conference—but the ground was really lit up by the brightness of the moon. And then the service started. The worship started, the dancing around the platform—you know just on a mud floor. And then all of sudden Jesus came and stood there in the sky, the moon was shining upon him, dressed in white, from the neck right down to the ankles, and his arms were reaching out to the people and that was the end of the preaching. The guy just mentioned Jesus—he was going to talk on the life of Jesus that night. Prepared the message but the moment he mentioned Jesus, Jesus came!

> He had to stop preaching. Because people were crying out. People were confessing their sins. They told me there were magistrates in the meeting who knew some of the people who were there, who they could never get to confess what they'd done in court, and they were actually hearing them confess what they did—that sort of thing was happening. Now the magistrates didn't go get a hold of them, because they were all taken up with what was happening. And Jesus remained there for quite some time. The meeting was over but God was moving, and bodies were being healed and people were set free from demon spirits you know and there was such a move of God.[115]

Our memories are malleable, and some of the details of a story told to Des twenty-nine years before, which in turn was recounting an event some fifteen years earlier can be questioned. But it's consistent with what Lano Longchar, who was there, reports about a meeting there in 1976:

> The whole town became like a big church and the sound of singing and praying was heard in every home. The revival finally culminated at Mokokchung football [soccer] ground which was attended by about 50 thousand people from all over Nagaland. It was a Wednesday night, around 10–11 p.m., the pandal [the stage covering] was

inaugurated. At that moment white doves came and sat above the pandal. The Friday night witnessed another miracle. A huge cross appeared in the pandal and Jesus appeared on the cross in different forms. Even non believers came from near and far and thousands got healed by the power of the Holy Spirit.[116]

While Longchar doesn't mention the confession of sins, he does go right on to give one evidence of repentance and change:

In one month's time only about a dozen cigarettes were sold from all over the shops. Two months later it was reported that no one bought at all. The real flame of revival had just begun.[117]

The phenomena of the natural creation being involved in spreading the word is consistent with something the Murry family knew about. Mhono remembered that during the '70s visitation, there was a group of Nepali woodcutters in the mountains near Wokha. "Nepali" is an umbrella term for a number of ethnic groups who share the Nepali language as their mother tongue. These weren't Naga tribesmen, but people staying in Nagaland for work; they would stay in the forest for months at a time. So while revival was going on in Wokha, "One day when they were cutting the wood, they heard music—singing—singing over the trees."[118] Needless to say the men were flabbergasted and ran into the town, where they found the same song being sung in the church service—a well-known Southern Gospel song with the chorus, "Jesus is coming soon, morning or night or noon." They heard the word of God and "that's how this Nepali church in Wokha town was born!"

Before we sigh, and wish we'd been there for this season of heaven touching earth, when the Commander-of-the-Universe made an inspection tour in the area of the Naga tribes, let's enlarge our account to include what was going on with Mhono during this period of revival. Mhono said emphatically: "At that time our family was in a very, very, very difficult situation. I was just like in hell. I was suffering so much. Mentally."

Interviewer: So the revival is going on but your life is hell?

Mhono: My husband, when he was quite young, he was revived. And struggling. He was struggling so much at that time. Whether to be in the service of God or to be in the government service? He was struggling SOOO much.

Ajano: Because when he got revived he knew that God called him—that's what he used to say. He knew that from the beginning, when the revival fire touched him, he knew then. He said he was disobedient, he should have left everything—but then he said, "But who will feed my children?" so he continued in the government service.

Mhono (at same time as Ajano): Not only that, before he got married, he had responsibility for his younger brothers and sisters. There was NO one to help them.

His daughter Ajano said her dad was "always disturbed" because he knew that God had called him, and that he was "going the opposite direction." So there was no peace in the rest of the family. That's partly why Mhono said "I was very much tortured mentally!" But it wasn't only Uncle Murry's struggle that made Mhono's life hell. At another time she explained more fully, when asked whether she had any happy memories:

So when I gave birth to a baby girl,[119] I was happy. I was happy because the baby was very cute—and I, I, stitched baby dress. The dress looked so nice on her. And I was happy to look at her but I used to live a very hard life. I didn't get—to be very frank in the sight of God—I didn't get much help from my husband also—inside the house. Outside though—he worked and he brought money for the family. And he loved his children also. But he did not know much about my hardship. Because of his simplicity.

One of the interviewers suggested this was due to the time period, which Mhono agreed with:

> In Naga culture, in the head-hunting age, whenever they go to the field—the men will be always at the back—with spear and dao[120] and weapons. Meanwhile, the babies, family supplies, vegetables, all these things will be carried by the women and the men will not carry ANYTHING. They used to carry dao, spear because if an enemy comes, they are ready to fight. That's why they did not help the women to carry anything.

Mhono said times and culture were changing, "But in our days it was not like that. So we (women) used to suffer so much." She went on to allude to both her physical and social condition: "Because I was weak as I told you when I was young I could not be happy. I could not bear the pressure."

But in the midst of her personal hell, our Lord was faithful to send comfort—this was Mhono's own personal experience of the wave of the Holy Spirit in the mid-'70s. In 1976, after Lano Longchar and his wife had been leading at a revival meeting in a nearby village, they came and visited the Murrys. They had connected previously through their joint hunger for revival.

> So they came and stopped at our house, prayed for us, and he told me: "Go and bring your Bible." Then I went, and brought my Bible. And she told me to open it to Jeremiah 29:11.[121] And she told me to read it out loud. So I read it out loud. And then he asked me, "Do you know what it means?" But I did not know. For what and for whom it is talking, I do not know. "No, I don't understand . . ." Then he explained it to me, "Your family has a future—don't be discouraged."

Indeed, the Murry family did have a future, but in meantime what was the fruit of this culminating wave of the Spirit in the broader Naga society? In a history of the Christian movement among another Naga tribe, the Zeliangrongs,[122] we see a picture of heaven on earth:

It was also reported that in 1978 the whole year, in the civil Hospital of Tamenglong District, there was not a single patient admitted except one or two police/military personnel.[123] It was also said that in the village of Tamenglong, in the year of 1979 not a single death occurred and no funeral service was conducted by the pastor. The whole area was experiencing peace, happiness and prosperity. There were no incidents of theft. There were no drunkards or smokers or social evils. It was the year of peace, calm and tranquility.[124]

To give some idea of the population involved, twelve years later in 1991 Tamenglong District had a population of 86,278.[125] The interviewers met a man from the same tribe, who remembered as a young child when his family became Christian in 1983. They were the last family in their village of Ntu, of about a thousand people, to become Christian—that is, "the last" as in "final, or complete." All the families in the village had become Christian![126]

This individual example of Ntu village must have been repeated again and again during this season. We can see this from the statistics for the whole state of Nagaland. The census of India asks people their religion; Christian is one of the choices. In 1981, after the "revival of love" among the Nagas, the percentage in Nagaland saying they were Christians reached 80.21%.[127] The growth to get to this point did take place over some decades. In 1941, Christians were 18% of the population of what would become Nagaland.[128] In 1951, this jumped to 46.5%. In 1961, after several years of atrocities and army occupation, Christian profession grew to 52.98%. In 1971 it climbed to 66.76%.[129]

We should mention that Mhono is skeptical of these statistics: "In Nagaland, 99% Christian but how many born-again Christians are there? Cannot say. Chinese, they can say. Koreans, they can say. . ." Keeping her skepticism about people claiming to be Christian but not really having a relationship with Jesus in mind, let's look for evidence of deeper commitment. Church membership is one specific evidence of Holy Spirit's work among a people, since it represents a specific commitment. The mid-1970s saw this grow in dramatic fashion. A Baptist leader's letter reported in July of 1978 there were "thousands of new converts, especially in the Konyak tribe where recently 20,000 have been added to the churches." He went on to say, "Opium has been a curse among the Konyaks but a great number of addicts have been cured and are now active in helping others."[130] Here's further details on this particular tribe: "In 1972, there were 25 churches and a total of 3,869 members." In 1977 there were 94 churches and a total membership of more than 30,000.[131] That's a better than sevenfold increase in five years!

This was greater than among most tribes, but the Holy Spirit's fire was touching all of Nagaland. There were 730 Baptist churches in 1972; in 1980 there were 1,197.[132] "The average size increased from 125 to 175."[133] To put this in other terms—between the first baptisms in 1872 until 1972, church membership grew to 91,250. In the next *eight* years, it more than doubled! Longkumer says: "More than a third of the Naga population is in active membership. More than two-thirds are considered Christian community."[134]

The church leaders had focused on revival in part as a means—to the goal of world evangelization. Just four days before Uncle Murry would be baptized by the Holy Spirit, on October 15, 1977, the president of the Nagaland Baptist Church Council, T. Alemmeren Ao, declared: "From today the task of world evangelization is started. NBCC [Nagaland Baptist Church Council] is enlisting 10,000 volunteers for the noble cause."[135] His statement would be followed by a general covenant with Christ to "dedicate our lives, talents, time and resources for the promotion of soul-winning ministry both inside and outside the land." This was signed by thirteen different tribal Baptist associations in 1981, and a further five were added in following years.[136]

Ponder and Apply

Then the devil took him to the holy city and set him on the pinnacle of the temple and said to him, "If you are the Son of God, throw yourself down, for it is written, "'He will command his angels concerning you,' and "'On their hands they will bear you up, lest you strike your foot against a stone.'" Jesus said to him, "Again it is written, 'You shall not put the Lord your God to the test.'" (*Matthew 4:5–7*)

The amazing visitation of God in Nagaland in the 1970s can lead to temptation: we can want to be part of the spectacular. This is the temptation the devil offered Jesus—to do something spectacular to prove His status. How do we keep our eyes on what our Lord is calling us to? Can we be content with the mundane? Are we willing to work and serve where we don't get any attention from others?

Henri Nouwen, in his wise book *In the Name of Jesus,* alerts us to this temptation. He addresses Christian leaders:

> When ministers and priests live their ministry mostly in their heads and relate to the Gospel as a set of valuable ideas to be announced, the [physical] body quickly takes revenge by screaming loudly for affection and intimacy. Christian leaders are called to live the Incarnation, that is, to live in the body—not only in their own bodies but also in the corporate body of the community, and to discover there the presence of the Holy Spirit. Confession and forgiveness are the disciplines by which spiritualization and carnality can be avoided and true incarnation lived. Through confession [to one another] the dark powers are taken out of their carnal isolation, brought into the light, and made visible to the community. Through forgiveness, they are disarmed and dispelled and a new integration between body and spirit is made possible.[137]

Besides resisting the flesh, we can step outside ourselves and join in God's mission. The Ao Baptist leadership focused on seeking God through the evangelization of the world. They consciously called their people to this grand purpose, deliberately and over time. Then Holy Spirit came with power and breadth.

CHAPTER 11

After Revival: Judgment or Wilderness?

You who have made me see many troubles and calamities will revive me again; from the depths of the earth you will bring me up again. (*Psalm 71:20*)

Students of revival will distinguish between the supernatural acts of the Lord and the effects they have on people as they live together—the social impact or reformation. Certainly there was community impact among the Naga tribes. But easy money and worldly temptations diluted the revival's continuing effects. This dynamic of revival followed by prosperity and decadence had also been also seen earlier. One of Uncle Murry's sisters, Chunbeno, reflected on the aftermath of the 1950s, and remembered that her brother's contemporaries from Okotso went on to become "doctors, engineers, architects." It was painful for my ears to hear her describe what she felt the village was like in the 1950s: "We were like pigs, and animals, and monkeys. We didn't know anything."

113

But she told how these residents of Okotso who'd grown up in the 1950s revival became "professional people." "So they want their children to get the best facility, the schools, the cars, and they started giving their children the best, everything the best." But unfortunately that dynamic brings with it great temptation—affluence hit the descendants of the Okotso revival hard: "The children become drug addicts, they are no more. So they couldn't keep on with the legacy . . . they didn't leave a spiritual heritage, many of them don't know God, they're just living like worldly people."[138]

The Murry children would grow up around the supernatural work of our Lord, including the revival of 1970s carrying into the early '80s. They were also watching human responses and efforts to sustain the move of God that would bring the revival into question. Uncle Murry's oldest son Thungbemo remembers wondering about people who were praying in tongues, when it would be one syllable repeated again and again: "dee-dee-dee-dee-dee-dee . . .". When he was 8 to 10 years old he sometimes went with his father as Uncle Murry led youth meetings: "Once they start praying in the Spirit there were all sorts of things—but one thing that I remember is firing at the devil: aka-aka-aka-aka," making a noise like machine-gun fire. Separately from that he also saw young people being slain in the Spirit: "Overnight they wouldn't wake up. They would just cover them up with a cloth and then they would just pray." As he remembered what he'd seen in those days, Thungbemo said that we "just can't figure out" people—he particularly meant the way different people respond to the Holy Spirit. He was quite disturbed remembering that two of the young men who were the most involved in the "firing at the devil" and spiritual warfare then went on to become gangsters. Eventually one was shot dead by the police, and the other later died of cancer.[139]

Each child's experience was affected by their age in relationship to the visitation of God. Ajano was born four years after Thungbemo, so by the time she remembers things there were still scheduled revival meetings every year—but the real power had gone. The experience of God was "watered down. When they confessed their sins, when they tell the truth, then they will start quarreling! Sometimes the people became so angry in the church" during these revival meetings. She even said the Murry children "were always scared" during these revival meeting times because of the mixture in the different kinds of manifestations. She believes the devil came and took advantage of people's fascination with revival and got them focused on "only trying to see visions" or having a prophecy—"they were only trying to manifest." She summed it up that people wanted to see miracles but not hear and receive the word of God. Both Mhono and Ajano were convinced there was one basic reason for the revival's lack of sustained impact: the lack of study and teaching in the word of God.

The Murrys' youngest son David was only three years old when his father was immersed in the Holy Spirit in 1977. He would add another element to Mhono and Ajano's focus on the lack of proper teaching: leadership was needed that could shepherd the people and "who knew the move of God, and understood the word of God, and could stoke the fire of revival." Of course, David added there are "very few people like that." David remembers the meetings of the 1980s:

> In those days prayer was really fervent. Honestly, lately, I haven't seen prayers like that. In those revival meetings, it was like what the Bible says about "the sound of many waters." When several hundred people come together and pray, it's amazing. . . . That's something that has stayed in my mind—I mean I was pretty young. I don't know about the preaching, I don't know much about the other things that went on, but the prayers—I can still hear them.

David remembers meetings in big tents, where thousands would gather with gas or kerosene lamps. "I would see mothers—mostly mothers— dancing around, singing; some of them had their eyes closed, they were just dancing back and forth in the Spirit."[140] By the time David was old enough to remember attending these meetings, his oldest sister was off at college. He does remember Ajano and his brothers presenting special musical numbers. David chronicles the effects of revival in his own life this way:

> For me personally, there were times when we went to those meetings when we felt the fear of the Lord. But as I grew up, I remember

going to this small Assemblies of God church and it was boring. So I suppose spiritual apathy was setting in and I would remember my dad preaching with tears in his eyes, his eyes closed. Sometimes he would literally cry. But I see, myself included, there was a lot of spiritual apathy after that. In our church there were a handful—20 to 30 believers. Of course, there were a lot of church splits also. The church split into . . . A-G 1 and A-G 2. The split is still going on.[141]

This split was in the 1980s, and unfortunately the pattern has continued, as A-G 2 split again in 2018.

My dad was a government servant; he would preach, he would exhort the people. Dad really had a heart for revival, he really had a heart for God—God had a strong grip on his heart. That you can tell. Looking back, Dad had always been this really intense person who was really going after God.

When he prayed you could always tell the zeal and passion in his heart. I think that made him miserable. His heart wasn't really in the government service. But he had to work, and he had to serve the government, and there was corruption in the government and I think that really made him miserable.

There was a time when he became a political victim and he was suspended from his job for five years[142] without pay. That was one of the darkest periods in our lives. All my siblings were at college. I was the only one at home during that [suspension] period. I think along that journey he was feeling like he was disobeying God the whole time.

During that time my oldest sister eloped.[143] I remember coming back from school and it was like a funeral at home—everything was like, dark; the news had come that my sister had run off. She was a medical student and she was doing really well and my parents were really proud of her. And she was a godly girl too; and I think those

things started making him realize that "I'm outside the will of God."
And then my brothers got into drugs, big time! It was like, one after
the other. Dark moment after dark moment. Mom was the only one
working at that time, so she was supporting all of us. It was really
difficult. My dad tried to do business, but everything was loss after
loss. So far as I remember, that was the darkest period in our lives,
in their lives.

I remember going to school and coming home—mom is locked
up in a room crying; and dad is in another room, locked up, crying.
I was a little boy at that time. I would come home and there would
be no food; because mom was sick with sorrow; dad, sometimes
out of grief he would just go into the jungle just to hunt, just to
get his mind off things. It was during that time, I believe, he started
reaching out to God, crying out to God. By God's grace, of course,
he, at the end of those five years, he was restored back to his service
but by that time, he had pretty much made up his mind that I'm not
going to do this for long—I'm going to serve God.

He attended several spiritual conferences. It was in one of the
Ralph Mahoney[144] conferences in Shillong[145] that he attended, that
he *really* felt like—this is it, God is calling. I think he was crying and
praying the whole night.

This call would have come in the mid to late 1980s. A few years later
Uncle Murry would retire early to start gospel work. David said the Murry
children had their questions about his decision, but David said, "I remember this very clearly—he told me several times—he said, 'God told me if
I take care of His business, He'll take care of my business.' That's what he
would often say to me. Meaning like the children, like all of us."

At that time my brothers were going crazy, they were all wild, doing
drugs. Ajano was in college. She was very rebellious at that time—
she eloped. I learned to fake it real well; I would be really naughty

but I saw how mom and dad were grieving; so whenever I was at home I pretended like I was an angel, just try to help them.[146]

Given the Murry family's experience, which is a common one in Naga society, it's sad to know that only some fifteen years earlier, Billy Graham had reported on his 1972 visit: "The Naga people also respect older people and take care of them. People here look forward to getting old because all the younger people respect them for their age. *There is little rebellion against parents as we know it in the Western world.*"[147]

Ponder and Apply

> So when they had come together, they asked him, "Lord, will you at this time restore the kingdom to Israel?" He said to them, "It is not for you to know times or seasons that the Father has fixed by his own authority. (*Acts 1:6–7*)

This is a biblical basis for seeing that God works differently at different times. There can be seasons of harvest, of consolidation and maturing, of mercy, of judgment. Nagaland's general experience can be played out in a person's individual life—after moments of great blessing, of supernatural unction or anointing, there can be times of temptation, testing, persecution, or even stagnancy. We can look at a divine act of judgment like what happened to Ananias and Sapphira and shake our heads in amazement: "How could they walk with so little fear of the Lord—particularly in that setting?" Yet we may do the equivalent (their heart sin was simply trying to look more generous than they were—lying) in a season of mercy and not realize it!

After Elijah's great triumph over the prophets of Baal on Mt. Carmel, he succumbed to fear when the queen, Jezebel, threatened his life. Extraordinary experiences of the Spirit are no guarantee we'll be protected from temptation, judgment, or wilderness experiences—even a short time later. Keeping the simple disciplines of intimacy with our Father, physical rest, and connection with other believers will help sustain us through those times.

CHAPTER 12

Trying to Walk Godly in Babylon

O LORD, who shall sojourn in your tent?
Who shall dwell on your holy hill?
He who walks blamelessly and does what is right
and speaks truth in his heart
. . . and does not take a bribe. (*Psalm 15:1–2, 5*)

Normal human dynamics certainly played a role in "corrupting" Nagaland as it went through the changes that come when tribal ways of bar-
tering and subsistence living encountered money, wealth accumulation,
commerce, and jobs with wages. In fact, Dr. J. H. Hutton, the British official
in charge of the Naga Hills District for years, could foresee the challenges
and spoke about them right after World War II at a conference on recon-
struction[148] in the area. He said the war and other events had greatly

> accelerated the rate of change, but have also laid upon the protect-
> ing power[149] a heavy obligation to see that the changes which are
> taking place shall be beneficial rather than detrimental. . . . The

danger is a very real one, for the general trend of the changes taking place is likely to involve a shift of influence from traditional village authorities to new men. . . . An economy based on cash currency . . . affords an immediate opportunity to individuals to amass personal fortunes and for a few to collect into their hands the means of production formerly distributed between many.[150]

Hutton studied Nagas for years in his work for the British government, and from 1917–1935 was the colonial officer in charge of the district. The tension between missionaries and colonizers was mentioned in the introduction, and Hutton certainly was an example of this tension. He was asked to judge a case in 1922 when Nagas following their ancient religious traditions were upset that idolatrous religious festival decorations had been cut down:

[T]hey demonstrated that on previous occasions it was the Christians and I have not the least doubt that it was Christians again this time . . . if these religious quarrels go on there will be nothing for it but to separate the Christians from the ancients entirely and forbid their going to each other's villages at all. I wonder why it is that it is so often the least pleasant of the community who turn Christians first. I suppose they stand the greater need of salvation.[151]

Whatever Hutton's opinions about the effects of missions, he accurately predicted the problems of economic change. These were increased as the central government of India poured money into Nagaland. Part of the government's effort to battle the independence forces was to buy off a good portion of the population. We recall when Mhono said it was so easy for her future husband to get a job in the 1950s. Mhono saw the overall process like this:

In Nagaland we can't produce ANYTHING. These days we are getting chicken and eggs and pigs, but in those days, we didn't produce

ANYTHING. Naga people just rely on government salary—from a Hindu country.

Besides the general social dynamics that go with a move from a tribal to a money economy, and an occupying army and government buying loyalty, there has been a spiritual force trying to overcome the amazing response to the good news. Certainly India is well known for corruption in government, but people like Uncle Murry will say Nagaland is worse than predominantly Hindu states in India for its level of corruption.[152]

What's a Jesus follower to do? Ajano remembers that because of her father's position as an executive engineer, people would constantly visit their house to ask for a job or a contract—and they would bring money, or if they didn't have money; vegetables or chickens.[153] Mhono chimed in to tell of two specific instances when her husband was in the Vigilance Department, where he did internal audits and investigations of government-financed building projects. One case involved a big building in the major Naga city of Dimapur; Uncle Murry took his son David with him to the city, who reported later what happened. The man involved came to Murry's hotel room and forced a bundle of money on him, as a bribe not to investigate the building's finances. Uncle Murry didn't keep the money, but took it back to one of the man's associates and told him to give it back to the man.

The other case Mhono remembered right off involved their own town of Wokha. During the dry season, Wokha suffers from a lack of water, so money was allocated to make a storage reservoir, except the contractor never did the work and received tens of millions of rupees. So Uncle Murry was sent to investigate this project, and again was met by a contractor with a bag of money. Uncle Murry refused the bribe and submitted his report. *The bribe then went to the official above Uncle Murry in the chain of command.*

Mhono went on: "He never took any bribe. He never made any false deals. That's why people didn't like him. 'If I make false deal, I share with you!' is the usual approach. But since he didn't do that, they said all kinds of evil against him. He suffered SOOOOO much." As Mhono said this, Ajano explained that her older sister had run into the same problems as an administrator at a government hospital—and thankfully was able to take the same strong stand for honesty. Ajano remembered how the families of men with the same rank in the government service as her father lived in affluence, with fancy cars and houses: "We used to feel ashamed, so ashamed"; most of their house was built in 1972 and could be considered unfinished fifty years later.

In Mhono's view, his refusal to take bribes was part of what made her husband a "misfit"—in the society, in church, in government work. Increasing the strain on her was that he wasn't content in his work—and struggling with the call to leave his job and serve God: "I spent my time in the school, and in the evening I come home. But when I come home, if I find anyone who isn't happy, always having a gloomy face, how can I be happy?"

Uncle Murry's continuing firsthand experience of corruption gives credibility to his strong words of warning to political leaders in a tract he published near the end of 1989.[154] Here's part of his warning:

> *God speaks to the political leaders:* Examine yourselves whether God's warning is true. . . . Your hunger for position and power has shed your brothers' blood. Your thirst for money has betrayed your sisters.[155] These two Satanic lusts have sold out your motherland. . . . You have brought political rum, the first Satanic weapon against our honest Christians. You have brought easy money, a stronger weapon against our simple citizens.[156]

Ponder and Apply

Thankfully, we may live in a situation where financial corruption isn't a constant temptation. But those who've been visited by the Spirit of God aren't just supposed to live with financially clean hands—we're to live with a generosity which outdoes the world. Are we sacrificial senders? Do we give to see the good news proclaimed among the unreached—at such a level that we feel pinched on occasion?

The temptations in our society may be more obvious in other arenas—how we use our tongues and our mental and emotional focus. Are we tempted to "keep up" with social media or news or entertainment? Are we discerning in how much time we focus on those when there are lonely hearts around us and a Father in heaven's heart looking for connection?

CHAPTER 13

Mission: One Fruit of Revival

Even if I preach the gospel, I can claim no credit for it; I cannot help myself; it would be agony for me not to preach. (*1 Corinthians 9:17, REB*)

It is striking that in all of our talks, Mhono never mentioned a personal revival experience of her own (other than the word of encouragement from a prophetic couple in 1976) but identified with the waves of Spirit entirely. Asked how their family still had a zeal for the Lord long after the revival, Mhono took a long time to think before answering:

From our childhood, we had been hearing: "God, God, God, salvation, salvation, salvation" . . . it has become a part of us. And as I was bringing up my kids I used to pray; early in the morning I would get up and just make the fire and by the fireside I came with their bodies in my hands and with tears I used to pray for them: "Lord we may not be able to do as much as you want us to do but when these children grow up, let them sing what we couldn't sing.

Let them say what we couldn't say. Let them pray, and let them do your work which we can't do." I prayed like that, I remember, when my husband was in the government service.

Only after my husband retired, then I'm very much satisfied. There was peace of mind in my life. And then, at least we can save some souls in a little bigger way. When he was in the government service, every year he took one month leave. And all the money he saved, he took and traveled all over India and held meetings and fed the people and then come back home.

So while his fellow government employees were getting nice cars or houses, Uncle Murry was investing his income in cross-cultural mission—taking the good news to other groups in the country of India. But Mhono wanted there to be some lasting fruit from this work:

I was thinking, "What if he does this every time?" There is no meaning—there must be some specific plan and program and ministry for him. So what to do? I was so much puzzled. But when he resigned from government service, I was very much at peace. And I thought that at least now we can find a certain line to work for God—and when we went to Sikkim I was very happy!

"From her childhood" Mhono wouldn't have just heard, but seen her father committed to preaching the word, not just among his own tribe, but taking it to other tribes as well. Even though his ministry was among Nagas, Merithung's work involved crossing language barriers.

Uncle Murry took early, voluntary retirement in 1990, shortly before he would have received a significant promotion. The retirement process takes time in their context. After some exploratory trips and ministry, and intense prayer and fasting for precise direction, Murry sensed a call to Sikkim where there were only a tiny number of professing Christians, and any existing churches were largely nominal. His son David told about launching out there:

Dad, Mom, Alan, and me, and Jiwan, a brother from Nepal; we had a Jeepsy. In those days the road was full of potholes and our journey—we made it to Guwahati—but from Guwahati to Siliguri was really difficult. We missed the way, wasted four hours. Finally to West Bengal—Melli.[157] It was past midnight—Mom wouldn't take it any more. Physically she was a little weak. Where do we go? Jiwan asked around and there was one Christian family, and they gave us a place to sleep that night, right by the river. At that point, they were like angels. My mom's condition was so worn out—we all just slept so well. In the morning they fed us so well! And they sent us on our way.

Dad had made some contacts in Sikkim. In Namchi we took a rented place with one Christian family—very, very nominal Christians but they gave Dad a rented place. We invited 30–40 young people and he would pray, worship with them, and teach them the word of God. Some of them were seriously demonized and they would manifest. *Thirty young people were set on fire—set on fire.* Dad would talk about what Samson did with the foxes. Dad would compare these young people to the foxes—and that's what they did. They went all over Sikkim. . . . When Dad first came, the Christian population was insignificant—but the Christian population exploded in the next five to ten years.[158]

From 1991 to 2001 the number of Christians as measured by the census of India went from 13,400 to 36,400. The growth continued, although at a slower rate, to 60,500 in 2011.[159]

Given that his spiritual formation was in a revival context, it's no surprise that this approach would shape how Uncle Murry conducted the training and his outreach ministry. Here's an account from his newsletter about the training class, complete with the detail that the fasting regimen he has proscribed was too strict for some:

In the middle of the third month, there was a test-revival week with three full days of fasting. Ten boys and five girls left as they couldn't go through the fasting days. We then selected a hilltop four kilometers away from Namchi and called it "Prayer Mountain." This spot is a beautiful hillock where the Government of Sikkim constructed a beautiful helipad, with a beautiful road connection. From this helipad we can see almost the four corners of Sikkim and Darjeeling town in clear view.

During those fasting days, we proceeded every early morning at 3:00 a.m. to this Prayer Mountain for consecrating prayers. After every praise and worship service as we arrived with unforgettable rejoicings together, we shook hands and dispersed to the jungles around for personal communication and contact with the Lord.

On every side, the sound of weeping, speaking in tongues, praising in spirit, prophesying, became the atmosphere in this prayer mountain. Nobody seemed willing to depart, feeling no hunger or thirst, desiring no more of old friends or their old life.

A rejoicing no less than was experienced by Peter, James and John in the company of Moses and Elijah together with the Lord Jesus. . . . In the afternoon we join up at the center of the prayer mountain, singing together as if we will never say goodbye. . . . [He then lists some of the English choruses and praise songs they sang.] Now, very often I faint to sing those songs, when I remember my children excitedly singing in the Spirit, some raising their hands, some with instruments, dancing and leaping, which exactly fulfilled the revelation given to me by the Lord, before I had gone there:

"Behold, thou shalt call a nation thou knowest not, and nations that knew not thee shall run unto thee because of the Lord thy God, and for the Holy One of Israel; for He hath glorified thee." (*Isaiah 55:5*)

After this unforgettable revival week and the wonderful experiences in Prayer Mountain we divided the students into several groups and sent them out into the remote places in Sikkim with the wonderful message of the Lord conducting revivals themselves.[160]

Mhono captures the personal side of the training in the same newsletter. We see the forty students who started had dwindled to seventeen by the finish, as she writes "Goodbye Sikkim":

He taught us how to serve Him in His power . . . even in the midst of adverse conditions and situation.

The most thrilling experience which we will never forget but yearn for throughout our lives was the warm, homey and lovely atmosphere. . . . when we started worshipping God, our neighbors, who were mostly Buddhists were so amazed by our voices. Even Jerusa, a small girl of 5 years old, the daughter of our good landlord, could not remain in bed in the early hours of the morning. It was terribly cold,[161] but . . . as soon as she heard our singing, she would jump out of the bed and just like a lark she would flap up to our flat to join us in the worship services. We found that without her, the meeting seemed to be incomplete.

These were the sweetest moments in our lives which we will never forget but we will cherish in our hearts. Most of our neighbors were Buddhists. They had never heard such singing before. So, some came to see us in amazement and became interested in our worship. They told us that they also have become Christians already.

During our stay in Sikkim people from all denominations co-operated with us. They extended their guidance and help to spread the gospel of Christ even to the remotest villages where vehicles could not reach. . . . Through their help my husband could go to many places and reach many people and God did miracles through him. Many got healing in their bodies as well as their spirits.[162]

After the Nagaland experience of division between believers, it's striking that Mhono could praise the cooperation between different types of believers. The newsletter does also feature a lengthy explanation of Uncle Murry guiding a believer to get baptized by immersion, since they'd only been baptized by sprinkling. (The initial missionary work in Sikkim was by Presbyterians, who practice infant baptism by sprinkling.)

Mhono's heart is evident as she talks more about how hard it was to leave:

Now the time had come for us to depart from these people of God. This was the most difficult time on our part. . . . On the evening of the 12th at 5:00 p.m. we held farewell meeting at the center. That meeting could not be concluded until 12 midnight. There was weeping, praying, praising, testifying, presentation and garlanding. It was a wonderful moment when the Holy Spirit dissolved all our hearts and precious tears of love and affection of the Lord rolled down from the cheeks of every person. Each of the seventeen students wanted to testify what the Good Lord had done in his/her life here at the center and how God changed his/her life now. Some of them were parentless and some were cast out of their homes by their parents for their acceptance of Christ. Both my husband and myself became just like their parents and our co-workers Daniel, Joseph and Ishmael Gurung became their brothers. There was a deep sense of love and affection among us and a strong cord of God's love bound us together which became so difficult to break off. They were weeping loudly and not to be comforted.

On the morning of the 13th some students went away to their homes and some students went directly to the field of God carrying only the Bible in their hands. As they went away from us, waving their hands to have a last glance until they disappeared out of sight—we could not control ourselves but also shed tears.

In poverty or in weakness both spiritual and physical, the voice of the Lord who called us for Sikkim lingers in our ears. That was the dynamic spiritual power which rejuvenates our spiritual life as we carry all our problems to Him. It is the secret of God that enabled us to pass through the seven months in Sikkim as one day.

Oh Sikkim, my husband and my children may see you again, but as for me, I feel it as if I journeyed to the moon along with my husband, never to see it again. I pray and hope I meet the precious jewels of Sikkim in the morning of the Lord, just inside the Eastern Gate. Sweet Sikkim—goodbye![163]

After this initial six-month training school, Uncle Murry did preaching campaigns in different towns. This was mainly, at first, in Sikkim. Mhono recalled how during one of those campaigns a leader of a rebel movement against the Indian authorities[164] had come to the city of Namchi in search of his only son, who had run away from home. The man saw a banner for the public meetings with the word "Harvest" on it—*so he thought it was an event put on by the Department of Agriculture.*

When this man came to the convention hall, the people were singing and praising God, very warmly—the presence of the Holy Spirit was there and so he was enthralled. . . . Then when he came inside conviction came to him, to his heart. So even before starting the program, when the praise and worship was going on, he went up to the pulpit and he confessed. Nobody told him to confess! "I am a murderer"—like that! He started in that way, "But now I confess all my sin, and I want to follow Jesus. I want to become a good man." The actual program was not yet started, but still he confessed. Then he said "My son ran away from home. I have searched everywhere but I cannot find him, so I am just going down to Siliguri [in the neighboring state of West Bengal], to find my son—so please pray for me." So the congregation prayed for him. And he went out and he came down to Siliguri. In those days, in Siliguri there was only one bridge over the Mahananda River, so there was ALWAYS a traffic jam there. So when he came, there was a traffic jam. And he was waiting and waiting and waiting. . . . At that time, he saw his son, sitting on a rickshaw, and coming towards him. So from there he just went and hugged his son! And they reconciled. They kissed. Then the father took his son and came up to Sikkim again, to Namchi, and testified in the meeting.

Mhono said the man went on to become "fully involved" in gospel ministry. Uncle Murry also held meetings throughout western Sikkim. He and his interpreter N. T. Lepcha would go out at 3:30 in the afternoon, and only return at 1:30 in the morning because so many people would want prayer in the meetings. Uncle Murry's mother tongue is Lotha, a Naga language. He would preach in English and be translated into the common language in the area, Nepali.

Mhono recalled one of many healings. This particular one happened in a village near the town of Sambaria, Sikkim. A paralyzed man in a needy family had offered 108 chickens (a magic number in Buddhist belief) to his god. But the invalid continued to be bedridden. Uncle Murry went and prayed for him, and he was completely healed. The villagers came in amazement, asking: "How could you be healed?" They proceeded to start following the true God as well. The healed paralytic went on to lead the church in that community.

Uncle Murry's ministry continued to mean travel back and forth from Nagaland to the Himalayan plateau. The travel had its challenges. One time Uncle Murry, his wife, and one son were traveling through Assam, during a military operation against rebel forces. Mhono remembers:

The military people were checking every vehicle. So we were stopped. We were carrying cash (for the ministry), more than 100,000 rupees in a briefcase, under some files and books. We start praying in our hearts—we could not talk to each other in front of them. "Oh God blind their eyes." A soldier opens the briefcase. One by one he is lifting things up. Now, he is about to reach the money. At that moment, another soldier came and tapped him on the shoulder, "Come, come," because it was time for a change in duties! He closed the briefcase and went away. Wonderful God! We escaped. Otherwise, if he had seen the money he would have taken all the money; and not only that, we would have been taken into custody.

This wasn't the only time their travels were a challenge, since driving to Sikkim from Nagaland meant crossing through another state:

One time David was driving the car, and when Assam police saw the Nagaland license plate, they tried to exploit us. They wanted money. These police will try to get money one way or another! We were passing through a checkpoint in Guwahati (a city in the state of Assam) and David was looking at the traffic policeman. He didn't raise his hand. Only when we came up close, he raised his hand. As soon as David saw the policeman's hand, he stopped. The policeman came and said, "Why didn't you stop?" David said, "I stopped when I saw your hand." Then came a false accusation: "You should have stopped back there." He took all the car documents and David's license. So we were sitting in the car and David didn't come quickly so Papa went. I was waiting in the car and just praying, just praying, just praying. After a long time I saw them coming back. If they had paid money, God had not answered my prayer. But if they didn't pay any money then God answered my prayer. As soon as they reached me I asked, "Did you give them money?" They said, "What money? Why should we give them money?" I was so happy!

One campaign which Mhono would describe as the zenith of Uncle Murry's ministry was in the town of Binnaguri, near the border of Bangladesh in West Bengal, India. Because it's a border area, there's an army base there. Often during his years of ministry Uncle Murry's own health was weak, but this time he was in full strength:

> So many sick people came. After the preaching, after the healing ministry is done, they didn't go away. They were running, dancing around, singing, clapping. . . . Sometimes they only left at 1:00 a.m. So many healings took place.
>
> Sanjib Sharma, he could not take a breath [through his nose due to nasal cancer], could only take breath by mouth, for a long time. He's the son of a Sharma, very high-caste Hindu. His father loved him so much, so he was given treatment everywhere but no cure. Then he came to this campaign. And he was healed! He could breathe through his nose! He testified over the microphone. Sanjib Sharma accepted Jesus Christ right there. And through him, so many people came to Christ. When he went home, his father expelled him from the house, because he was healed! *(laughter)* So we took him with us.

The Murrys ended up sending Sanjib to a Bible school in nearby Darjeeling, West Bengal. Mhono had worked with the leader of the Bible school, David Mangratee,[165] years before in Wokha, when the Murrys were first married. Mangratee had then moved to Darjeeling, where he started a ministry, a church, and eventually this Bible school. Since Sanjib had been kicked out of his home, Mhono said he had only one top to wear! "No extra clothes, no bedding, nothing. So we gave him all the necessary things," and provided for him to go to the Bible school for a year. "Then we took him to Nagaland and we put him in Kohima Bible College[166] for two years." During his Bible school training he learned to speak English fluently, on top of his Hindi and Nepali. Sanjib went on to open a Bible school himself and has become a prominent ministry speaker.

At this point the interviewer asked Mhono about a son-in-law's memory of the Binnaguri campaign: On the first night the police told Uncle Murry not to pray in Jesus's name—not only that, but the officials also showed up for the first meeting, came up on the stage, and sat in the VIP chairs! So Uncle Murry prayed, "What shall I do?" He decided to pray in the name of the Creator God to open the meeting. The moment he did so, all the policemen fell out under the influence of the Spirit, right on the stage, and they remained unaware for the entire meeting. At the end of the evening they roused themselves and said it had been a good meeting, and went home and didn't return the other nights! After having her memory jogged, Mhono remembered it this way:

> Police came just for investigation and observation, to find fault. But when he prayed in the name of Jesus, all of them—not just police, but all the congregation, were slain in the Spirit—fell down, just like wind came. Yeah, that also happened. I didn't remember, but just now as you say that, I remember. And the military officers who were there, they were very happy. They started dancing, and singing and clapping hands—they were seated on the platform—they enjoyed it with us. After that we could go to Army commissary and get things at a cheaper price! They invited us to do that.

Mhono continued reminiscing about this period of Uncle Murry's life when he was strong. Her father Merithung helped them finance a series of outreach meetings in Jaigaon, on the Bhutan border. Bhutan was, at that point, an absolute monarchy allied with the Buddhist religious structure (the country only had their first elected parliament in 2004, and the king is still immensely powerful).[167] One family from the kings' court came to their meeting.

> This noble's wife had studied in the USA. She had a double PhD. They brought their two sons, and ate food with us. Very simple food. Plain rice and dal[168] and vegetables. They enjoyed our food.

And this nobleman said, because the preacher preached about the New Jerusalem, the kingdom of heaven, the new heaven and the new earth, he was overjoyed. "The nations of the earth will eat the leaves of the tree of life for healing." His friend is a good Christian. So the nobleman was just joking, "Okay, I will not be in the New Jerusalem in heaven, but my friend will be there in the New Jerusalem, so every month he will pluck fruit from the tree of life and he will send me some. I will get only the leaves but he will send me the fruit!"

Mhono doesn't know if he became a Christian, as personal communication at that time consisted of written letters—no internet and social media. And the post "would take months to reach us."

Uncle Murry continued the mission, many times apart from his wife who was still working as a teacher in Wokha, Nagaland. He was led to locate a mission base outside Siliguri, West Bengal, in the adjoining town of Milan More. Some idea of their lives is captured in a letter of uncertain date, possibly 2001, from Mhono to him there. She wrote entirely in English:

My dearest,

Received your letter and I am really amazed for the protecting hand of the Lord and praised His holy name. He is our Shepherd. . . [then some lines on her concern for Ajano and news about Alan].

I am so much concerned for you but I cannot do anything. I just continue to uphold you in my prayers just as Aaron and Hur in the olden days helped Moses in lifting up his hands to overcome their enemy. I know your weaknesses and you also know my weaknesses. But God might have chosen the weak vessels to shame the strong people. So let us not give up. Simply surrender yourself in the mighty hands of the Lord and just feel at ease, feel yourself comfortable and feel relaxed. Don't push yourself too much but just trust in the Lord.[169]

Prabha Baraik remembers those days with Uncle Murry in Milan More. As a young girl of 11 or 12 she met them because the Baraiks' home was at the edge of a village of tea garden workers. Their home was one of the first dwellings on the road east of the property Uncle Murry had finally been able to obtain in Milan More, on the edge of the tea garden.[170] Prabha remembers:

> We used to have flowers by our gate and his wife really liked the flowers. And she asked, "Hey, can you give me these flower branches so I can plant some at my house?" And we said yeah, sure, and she came to our house. Then we found out she's Christian, so we welcomed her . . . and that's how we got to know her. And then we gave her the flower—she really liked it and she planted it.[171]

Their communication was definitely cross-cultural. Prabha explained that Uncle Murry knew some Hindi: "He knew some basic words, like 'eat' or 'come' or 'let's pray,' that kind of thing. And he would pray in his dialect. They knew a little Hindi, just broken Hindi, but we knew what they're trying to say, and that's how we used to communicate." Uncle Murry's spiritual devotion was obvious even to an 11-year-old:

> He used to go in the hills and I know he used to do fasting and praying and walking. He loved to pray for people. He was always available for people. Even though we have different culture or language, he loved to pray for us.[172]

After that initial meeting, Prabha remembers:

> My parents went to visit him for prayer. That's how they got to know them. Since they [the Murrys] didn't know anybody [in the community], they asked my dad if he could guard the property while they were going to be away in Nagaland. They knew us through the flowers, so we said okay, because it's good that my dad can get a little

more money. So my dad used to go there every night, watching the property and that's how we got to know them.[173]

Prabha and her mother were Christians, but her dad wasn't yet—he came to the Lord in 2007.

Deepak Kuswar was a young man reached in the Murrys' ministry in Milan More. He remembered that when Uncle Murry was there: "The environment of the compound was of peace and calm—it was completely different than the outside. As you entered gate you feel the presence of God. You feel GOOD!"[174] He also remembered Uncle Murry's outreach work: "I attended one of his revival meetings in Nagri, which is up in the hills, near Darjeeling. I saw in that meeting many people were being brought by jeep from hospital." He said many of those received healing.[175] Ajano remembers Uncle Murry leading the local believers on prayer marches around their area—sometimes at 3:00 in the morning![176]

Besides the dramatic shift in the spiritual climate of Sikkim, Darjeeling district, and Bhutan, Uncle Murry's lasting legacy is the training center he founded in Milan More. He discovered that people he'd led to the Lord weren't being trained in the ways of God in their traditional churches. When he visited them again, he heard, "Uncle, we were blessed, we were healed, we were born again during the crusade and we went to the local churches as you have told us to do but we still don't know how to pray."

A hallmark of Uncle Murry's training was the practice of intense prayer and fasting. As mentioned in the introduction, this is what caught my attention. Here's the details one participant remembers about the two-hour evening prayer meetings:

Once he starts praying he will forget everything else. One of the songs we used to sing was: "So forget about yourself, concentrate on Him and worship Him—Worship Him, Christ the Lord." That forgetting about himself, that was exactly what he did. He just forgot everything and his prayer was always concentrated on this word "revival." Just "revival." Awakening. The latter rain. And he would pray non-stop for it, the movement of God. And we—young people—we would sometimes fall asleep. He could sit on his knees—and pray for two hours non-stop—it was amazing! But then we would go to sleep and sometimes in the middle of the night, if we had to go to the bathroom we had to go outside because there was a toilet outside. So we'd go and we'd see there's still light in his room, and we can still hear him, singing some melodies, or hear him in prayer, or see that he was searching the scriptures. Something kept him awake—but he would be the first one to rise in the morning also! It's not like he had a lack of sleep—I think he ate and drank revival.[177]

Ajano remembered being alarmed one time later when her father had fasted for forty days at a prayer center in Kurseong, near Darjeeling, and he was so weak when he came back to their base in Siliguri that she had to nurse him through recovery. Another time, she said, he did forty days at a prayer center in Chathe, Nagaland. One of his sons saw him from a distance afterward, and their dad was so thin he didn't recognize him. It may have been during the same trip, when returning to Wokha, that a relative of Yaniethung's saw them and said to Mhono, "You should take care of your husband." She was so embarrassed.[178]

Even as this book is being written, Uncle Murry continues to pray for revival and missions at his home in Wokha, Nagaland and sing to our Lord! The training center continues in Siliguri, and offers both a short course brought to other locations, like remote villages, as well as a two-year practical training course at the center. The training course at the center is composed of four teaching terms with lengthy practical ministry experience between each term.[179]

Ponder and Apply

Not everyone is called to be an ambassador for Jesus in another culture. Not everyone is called to move locations to follow Christ. But have we asked: "Lord, what do You want to do with my life?" Are we open to the possibility?

Given the costs to make such moves, more senders are needed than "go-ers." Is there a rule-of-thumb ratio—perhaps twenty households sending for each one that's sent? Of course there are variations and different possibilities within these two basic roles. Going as a self-supported ambassador, making your living in another place, another culture, may be your calling. Or you could serve by staying where you are but overcoming cultural barriers by welcoming those from other places—and looking for opportunities to share Jesus with them.

In one way, it's unfortunate the label "Great Commission" has been fastened on to Jesus's parting words in Matthew 28:18–20. He instructed us to make learners or disciples as we're going, teaching them to obey what Jesus taught. When it's identified as a "commission" it can be seen as a "task"—one item on a to-do list. Yet, His words are really about relationship—because He's in charge of the world, He's doing this—and He will be with us as we do it with Him. *So when we hear "Great Commission," let's mentally relabel it "Great Relationship"—as a step to living the revived life.*

PART 2

Exploring Details of God's Move

As we've moved through this account of Holy Spirit's work among one Naga family, in the midst of the larger visitation in the different Naga tribes, there are topics which deserve further exploration. With the basic history in mind, let's now look at some specific topics in more depth.

CHAPTER 14

How Does Revival Start? (Part II)

All these with one accord were devoting themselves to prayer. . . . And suddenly there came from heaven . . . (*Acts 1:14a, 2:2a*)

Philip went down to . . . Samaria and proclaimed to them the Christ. . . . And the crowds with one accord paid attention to what was being said. . . . So there was much joy in that city. (*Acts 8:5–6, 8*)

Instead of our title question, we could ask: When does revival begin? Is it the "suddenly"? Or the ten days of united prayer beforehand? Does it start with the preaching, or with the response of great joy in the city?

Merithung wrote his thoughts on the topic. His brief view of the 1950s was written in 2002, late in his life—looking back on events which happened before he was actually following our Lord:

Meanwhile the Lord God in heaven determined to build up the body of His Son Jesus and He moved His servants, the foreign

missionaries to proclaim a revival week. Accordingly they proclaimed it, March-April 1952 through Assam, Manipur and Naga
Hills districts. Yes, a mighty revival broke out in the interior
churches and the Holy Spirit baptism was manifested in simple
believers, speaking in tongues, casting out satan and healing the
sick. The church leaders were terribly frightened and they quenched
the church flame. This foolish act of the church leaders invoked the
wrath of the Lord God. He punished the Nagas under the heavy
hand of the Indian army who burnt down their dwelling places and
granaries, raped even minor girls mercilessly, gathered together the
younger mothers in church buildings and treated them in horrible
and shameful manner defiling the holy places of worship.

In those days many pregnant mothers who escaped were roam-
ing in thick mountain jungles seeking shelter in caves under rocks
and therein gave birth to babies and for lack of care many of them
died along with the babes.

Nevertheless there were remnants of the past revival who cried
out in tears to God day and night. Hearing their prayers the Lord
God remembered His people once again and sent another wave
of revival which took place in the Ao and Lotha areas in the same
manner on the day of Pentecost. Soon after it broke out in Kohima
district[180] in greater extension covering the district and its neighboring villages.[181]

Merithung's account covers decades—the initial revival went several
years, and the military occupation began in 1954. The remnants of the past
revival crying out in tears refers to the groups that gathered in the 1960s
and early '70s. While Merithung viewed the atrocities as God's judgment,
it's also possible to see that God sent a wave of mercy in anticipation of the
Nagas' suffering.

For those looking for more natural explanations, were there social conditions that contributed to God's supernatural work? One of Uncle Murry's

sons-in-law thinks the innocence of the Nagas made room for revival. "There was no guile" among them, were his words. Certainly one can see this in Uncle Murry.

As an additional although not necessarily contradictory view, the key academic paper about the revivals in Nagaland available in the West noted that the revival's beginnings came when the Naga tribal churches were at a low ebb spiritually after World War II. The paper quotes one source, "There were more backsliders in the Church than genuine believers."[182]

> It was in such a spiritual decline that some churches in Nagaland experienced a movement of the Spirit during 1948–1952. This movement took place in two stages under two different men. The first stage of local revival was under the ministry of C. E. Hunter, who was then the administrator of the mission station at Impur.[183]

The academic quotes the second man, evangelist Rikum, as saying about Hunter that he was "filled with the Holy Spirit. He saw the Christians, having been baptized without receiving the Holy Spirit, as heading towards hell. Therefore, he cried silently and at other times aloud. I was filled by the same love through the Holy Spirit, and looking at the sinfulness of the Nagas, I wept."[184] Since we know of Rikum's key role in the '50s revival, this statement about what inspired him deserves great attention. What did Hunter mean in saying that "Christians, having been baptized without receiving the Holy Spirit," were headed to hell?

Hunter refers to his own doctrinal beliefs in a letter sent during that time period to his mission supervisor. He was answering a question from a couple of potential supporting churches who wanted to know his doctrinal position. In the letter he asked his supervisor at the U.S. headquarters to send the church committees a doctrinal statement from his files because he had only a little space in his aerogram letter:[185]

> I mentioned the 1,100 (approx.) baptisms of last year, and told of the intensive effort we are making with three full-time translators to

give the Word of God to the people in their own tongue. I thought it much better to report the RESULTS OF SOUND CHRISTIAN FAITH AND EVANGELISM THAN TO MERELY GIVE DOC-TRINAL PROPOSITIONS.... [S]ome committees want a rather full statement. My faith has grown and my understanding of the Christian faith has deepened and expanded, but my position is the same as in the year of my appointment. You may use that statement freely with churches interested in supporting us. I am no hyper-Fundamentalist of dispensational views and millennial hobbies, and do not care for the support of such churches. But I have no time for modernism, only for the faith of the New Testament. I take it that by and large I am typical of many, many Baptists which in a measure I represent out here. More than that I want especially to be true to Christ whose ambassador I was commissioned to be.[186]

Although Rikum's words that Hunter was "filled with the Spirit" could be understood by a charismatic or Pentecostal as referring to a particular experience of Holy Spirit, that's not necessarily intended. And Hunter's words that his faith has "deepened" could refer to a deeper understanding of the Holy Spirit's present work in believers. Still, the simplest explanation of Rikum's words is that Hunter was concerned about blatant lukewarmness and nominalism among the believers—that following water baptism there was no evidence of following Christ. In chapter 20, "Revival and Division," we'll see that a key point of contention would be: Should a person repent and believe before being water-baptized? This seems basic, but remember Uncle Murry's own testimony—immediately after his own water baptism he stole from his neighbor! And Merithung had been water-baptized without believing.

Longkumer gives details of how Hunter and others went about seeing the ground prepared for a change in heart among the believers:

Many church leaders shared Hunter's concern about the low spiritual condition of the church. Prayers for a revival began all over the churches after the Naga Baptist Church Association Golden Jubilee celebration in January, 1947, with great effect. The following steps were taken as preparing for revival:

1. About a hundred revival hymns such as "Revive Us Again" and "O Lord, Send a Great Revival," were translated from English into Ao Naga.
2. All Ao church leaders met together in the Mission Center at Impur for Bible study and prayer.
3. During these meetings, the revival songs became popularized.
4. Following the meetings at Impur, weekly neighborhood prayer fellowships were conducted in every local church.

It was during these prayer meetings that the Spirit of God started to move in the hearts of the people. People began to pray in deep conviction of sin. Many rededicated their lives to Christ. Individuals who had been excluded from fellowship came back to the church. Some old habits such as smoking, chewing pan and the like, were given up by those addicted.[187]

Church leaders from the Ao tribe went in twenty-five different teams to evangelize among other Naga tribes during 1949 and 1950.[188] Longkumer's history goes on to say:

Hunter had to leave Nagaland in 1950, due to some personal problems. He was succeeded by A. S. Truxton. In 1952, a somewhat phenomenal revival broke out in some villages under the fiery preaching of the young Rikum. Rikum was a close associate of Hunter and had the same burden for the spiritual poverty of the Nagas.[189]

Hunter wrote a report as he was returning at the end of 1950 to the USA. Before we look at what these "personal problems" involved, let's look at some things Hunter reported with the advantage of hindsight.

His words are pregnant with meaning, as his list of happenings for the year includes:

> Educational and promotional meetings included two Bible con-
> ferences for Ao's at Impur of exceptional spiritual power and high
> attendance. A course for unlicensed pastors was held there also, and
> a very interesting pastor's conference.[190]

The words "very interesting" are so intriguing—again with the advantage of hindsight. Hunter had started out his report:

> OUTSTANDING ACHIEVEMENTS IN 1950: This has been the
> most outstanding year in the Impur field in many ways. In evange-
> lism this year not only have more souls been won to Christ in the
> seven tribes of this field than in any previous year, a total of 2750,
> but the intensity of evangelistic fervor and scope of soul-winning
> activity have been greater than ever before.[191]

In this next paragraph we catch some of Hunter's concern and passion. We can ponder—what did he mean by the term "revival"?

> URGENT NEEDS FOR THE FUTURE: Although during the
> past three years of emphasis upon revival and soul-winning many
> churches have experienced an awakening, this is not true of some
> weak churches, where there is still much need for revival. The two
> Ao evangelists should major upon revival of such churches.

He goes on to give detailed concerns about the situation in each of the seven tribes their mission station was working to reach, and sugges- tions for staffing and translation work. We can wonder if Hunter would have known of a much earlier predecessor's report of "the first revival in the Naga Hills" in 1896, more than fifty years earlier. The original missionaries to the Nagas, Edward and Mary Clark, had witnessed the start and then the decline of a church among the Ao tribe. The decline was due to some bad decisions by a couple of the Clarks' teammates. But then fortunately, a couple of Naga leaders, notably Kilep and Zilli, were able to reverse the bad decisions, make some changes and continue presenting the gospel in such a way they revitalized the infant church and saw a "large number" become believers.[192] In that sense, Hunter was redigging a well of revival in his passion!

But the true depth of Hunter's passion is told in his widow's words! The "personal problems" were that Hunter had worked himself to death. Shortly after writing his report, while on the ship from Kolkata to Canada, before the ship reached Aden, in Arabia, on December 24, 1950, C. E. Hunter died at age 40 of coronary thrombosis.[193] His body never reached the United States, as he was buried at sea. Within a few weeks of his death, his widow Cleda had the presence of mind to write to the mission board secretary about her late husband:

> As Kijungluba, the Ao evangelist, wrote to me, "He gave himself unreservedly for the glory of God's kingdom and his work and service will speak to the people forever!" George Supplee wrote: "No doubt his arduous labors for the people contributed to the attack that took him away." He did work day and night—as if he had only a little while to do all the things he wanted to do. Though we both knew he wasn't well, we thought it was only the repeated attacks of dysentery which we had both had. Because he was so very tired I begged him to rest and relax on our trip home: but he always said he was all right and he wanted to finish typing the manuscript for the printers. He did finish the Konyak work which he had with him and sent it to the printers in Kolkata from Bombay. He had started the typing of (the gospel of) Mark in Sangtam.[194]

We know Rikum was much affected by Hunter's passion. We can see in Hunter's life the death of a seed leading to a harvest as Longkumer goes on to describe the beginning of what overwhelmed Okotso village:

After his return from Bible College, Rikum began his preaching ministry. In his preaching, the main emphasis was on sin, confession, prayer and the Holy Spirit. While he preached, people began to feel deep conviction of sin and started to pray aloud, confessing their sin.

As people continued to pray, some saw visions and some spoke in tongues. This caused some confusion among the church members. Ao Church Association leaders became alarmed and tried to stop the movement. There was a fear that "such a movement might cause division in the unity of Baptist churches in Nagaland." Meantime, a Pastor Benjamin from an extreme Pentecostal background came preaching in Nagaland. He won some followers, who were re-baptized by him.

One of them was an Ao from Longkum village who began a separate movement in his church; this brought further confusion to the revival movement. Rikum was given orders by the church council not to preach and was for some time suspended from his work; after further investigation, he was reappointed to Ao Baptist Church Association work at Impur. Thus, the revival in the Ao area was stopped; however, it spread to other tribes, such as Angamis, Rengmas, Lothas, Chakhesangs and Southern Semas, spontaneously.[195]

So did the revival begin in the despair in Hunter's heart which in turn inspired Rikum? Did the preparations Longkumer lists cultivate hunger among believers? How does one account for its "spontaneous" spread?

At least from Mhono's view, Rikum's pursuit of the Holy Spirit was a key factor in bringing the supernatural work of God to Nagaland. Mhono remembered Rikum's path intersecting with that of Oral Roberts—who she said had come to India, been frustrated at his lack of power, went back to the USA, and then returned with power which he passed on to people like Rikum. Since there's no record of Oral Roberts being involved in India during the late 1940s, it's possible she's remembering a different healing evangelist, T. L. Osborn. Her description of the evangelist initially having no power in India certainly fits Osborn's own words. He summed up his experience in a book which is now difficult to access: *Frontier Evangelism: God's Indispensable Method for World Evangelism,* published in 1955:

> I know what it is to be "a reproach" among the heathen. Before I knew about God's will to heal, I served in India as a missionary. It was in 1946. I was challenged by a Mohammedan to prove that Jesus Christ was the Son of God and that He had risen from the dead. I could not do it. No miracles were happening in my ministry. I preached but there was no evidence. But in 1947, God showed me "the power of His works." What for? That I might no more be "a reproach among the heathen," neither in India, America, nor in any other country of the world.[196]

Osborn and his wife then went on pursuing a ministry of healing and the miraculous around the world, beginning, according to his book, in Jamaica in 1949. His daughter says he didn't visit India again until 1959.[197] So who *did* pray for Rikum around 1950?

David Murry has thought much about how God moved in Nagaland and connects the move in the 1950s with a different city in India from the one his mother mentioned—not Allahabad, but Hyderabad:[198]

> And then I heard my dad tell me about one man—early days, maybe right after World War II. He was a Baptist—in those days Baptist was all we had. He came preaching a very different message than what the Baptists were preaching. He told me the name of that man, but I forgot the name.
>
> He was Naga—before Rikum. I think Rikum was mentored by this earlier man but he got this fire in Hyderabad. The Hyderabad mission, was an offshoot from the Azusa Street revival! Amazing! So seriously, the fiery spark spread and it reached Nagaland. But

this man, according to my dad, this man was different. He was not what you would call a Pentecostal preacher, he was different from the typical Baptist preachers, so he kind of stirred things up. I think he even came to Okotso in those days, and he was like a circuit preacher.

My mother's side of the family, my grandfather, was so touched and impacted by the revival so deeply. They were products of the early '50s revival. So the '50s revival had impact from the Azusa Street revival.

He lamented the people he knew who had experienced the fire of God, but because of a lack of relevant teaching didn't have an understanding of the word: "Eventually the fire died down, and you don't see a passion for God anymore." David Murry shared a couple of other names that played a role in stoking the fires of revival:

My dad was deeply impacted by Ralph Mahoney's preaching and teaching and his articles. I'm sure you have heard of *The Shepherd's Staff*?[199] So my dad studied that a lot. And he would subscribe to magazines, like *Voice of Healing*, Gordon Lindsay's magazine. Those things were basically his feeding, because in the churches in those days the preaching and teaching of the word of God was, if I may say, very, very minimal!

The Assemblies of God had a big part in the revival movement in those days. I remember Mom and Dad used to talk about Rev. Mark Buntain. I heard that name so many times. And he would get people from Kolkata to come preach in our church and put on revival meetings. I think he played a big role in birthing revival from what I have heard, I personally didn't know him, he was an amazing man of God, he was a true pioneer in India, pioneer in the faith. The movement in our part of the world—Rev. Mark Buntain had a lot to do with it.[200]

Besides working through individuals who pray and anoint other individuals, whether a T. L. Osborn or someone from Azusa Street, a case can be made that our Lord works in seasons. There are similar reports of His work in different geographical places in the same time period. For instance, starting in 1948, there was an outbreak of the supernatural, most prominently in Saskatchewan, Canada, which became known as "the Latter Rain Movement." The earliest significant outbreaks among the Naga tribes appear to be sometime in 1952. The "Voice of Healing" movement in the United States was certainly underway by then as well.

While all discussion of revival has to eventually accept the mystery of Holy Spirit's coming and going where He does like the wind, certainly humans are involved in not quenching the wind, not grieving the Spirit. When we consider this aspect of revival, the nature of *and* the response to the teaching appear to be important. For instance, earlier in the chapter we noted Rikum's focus in his preaching in 1952 was described as "sin, confession, prayer, and the Holy Spirit." The Okotso Baptist Church jubilee booklet recounts the beginning of the '50s wave of the Spirit:

> Mr. Rikum Ao, while in Allahabad, received new life through revival, and when he came back to Nagaland in 1952, he conducted revival meetings, by sharing the word of God, pointing to the people of Longkhüm and Mangmetong about sin and salvation. Many people who were touched by the Holy Spirit, confessed their sins and received new life in Christ. At this juncture, some women folk from Okotso went and attended the meetings at Mangmetong. They too were convicted of their sins and accepted Jesus by confessing their sin. Pastor Phandeo took with him the church treasurer and attended the meetings at Mangmetong. He found that the teachings of Rikum were based on the leading of the Holy Spirit about new life. He and his companion joined the women folk and thus the church of Okotso was flooded with the power of God and the church was transformed in no time.[201]

Rikum's passion and teaching are important—but so is Pastor Phandeo's willingness to respond and open the door for him to teach! There are further allusions in Okotso Baptist Church's history to the work of the Spirit in that season. The village's first pastor, Etisassao,[202] served from the beginnings of the church in 1904 until 1912 when he was "compelled" into British government service. He was then sent to work along with a couple of thousand other Nagas in the British war effort in France in World War I. "He had been in government service and retired around 1928, and settled in the village [Okotso] permanently. His faith was wonderfully renewed in 1952–1954 when revival swept through the churches in Nagaland like wildfire. He was called back home by the Lord on April 10, 1967 at the age of 110."[203] The account goes on to say of the church as a whole, "Gradually believers were added and by 1953, through Holy Spirit's revival all villagers were converted, and thus became the first Christian village in Lotha territory."[204] The challenges of revival are also mentioned in the history booklet. We'll explore this further in chapter 20, "Revival and Division."

Ponder and Apply

As we explore some of the themes that emerge from looking at this history of Holy Spirit's work among the Naga tribes, we should allow their history to call all of us upward and onward.

There is a route forward into more of the Holy Spirit. On the one hand, reading about the Mozhuis and Murrys should sober us about the sacrifice and cost involved in revival. On the other hand, the whole idea of a visitation of God should be more immediate and accessible as we consider their history. These are normal people, leading normal lives, who were touched and changed by the Holy One of Israel. While their community and the trauma their society went through may seem so different on the surface, there are similarities of heart and human experience that allow us to identify with these very human vessels of God's glory.

If I was to zero in on one thing, I would see the passion represented by weeping, even in just a few people praying, as a key. We can see this biblically:

Those who sow in tears shall reap with shouts of joy! He who goes out weeping, bearing the seed for sowing, shall come home with shouts of joy, bringing his sheaves with him. (*Psalm 126:5–6*)

I don't know any farmers who weep as they plant their crops. This is talking about the weeping of people planting spiritual seed with their passion—like Hunter and Rikum. It's the pattern the prophet Joel describes:

Let the priests, who minister to the Lord, weep between the porch and the altar; let them say, "Spare Your people, O Lord." (*Joel 2:17a, NKJV*)

We believers are the priests—the ones who can weep in between the world and the meeting place with God. I had the privilege of hearing Lou Engle (who wrote the Foreword) ask this compelling question in a prayer meeting: "How will the unbelievers hear—unless we weep?" May this question be stamped on our spiritual eyeballs! Joel goes on to describe the answer to the weeping prayer between the porch and the altar:

Then the Lord will be zealous for His land, and pity His people. The Lord will answer and say to His people, "Behold, I will send you grain and new wine and oil, and you will be satisfied by them; I will no longer make you a reproach among the nations. (*Joel 2:18–19, NKJV*)

A harvest of grain, new wine, and oil certainly represents spiritual harvest and refreshing—in a word, a visitation of God.

The families we're following weren't passive. They responded to God and then pursued Him. They lived up to what they'd seen: "Only let us live up to what we have already attained" (*Philippians 3:16, NIV*).

What does this involve? We can:

- Seek out those people with greater Holy Spirit activity in their lives and ask them to pray for us, to anoint us! Just as Rikum Ao evidently did.

- Make decisions and plan for increasing the awareness and desire for a visitation among our circle—whatever circle that is. Whether it was the missionary C. Earl Hunter's deliberate approach to plan meetings and prayer campaigns (combined with his passion that meant he gave his life in service to the Nagas), or the Ao Baptists mapping out a plan for increasing the spiritual life of their groups and churches—human decisions can be involved in sowing the seeds.

God will respond to the hunger of His people—we can be sure of that.

At the same time, our relationship in asking for more of Him isn't a formula. This particular follow-up to the 1857–58 awakening in the United States may represent others:

> Dr. Girardeau frequently referred to this [the 1857–58 awakening] as the Lord's mercy in gathering His elect for the great war that was so soon to sweep so many of them into eternity. . . . After the war another great effort was made to secure a revival of the same kind. A sunrise prayer-meeting was organized for the sole purpose of praying for such a work of grace, and although the people went into it with great enthusiasms and high expectations, after several months of earnest and persistent effort many of them began to cease their attendance. Some with stronger faith continued for a year before becoming discouraged and finally, giving up hope. In speaking of this great struggle, Dr. Girardeau was accustomed to say, "God is sovereign."[205]

When there are disappointments with God, we can still "live up to what we have attained." Whether it's the difficult work of appearing to be divisive by continuing to teach the present-day work of the Holy Spirit, like Merithung and his companions did during the 1960s, or the simple joy of continuing to pray in private after being touched by the Spirit, remnants can sustain revival fire—and see the fire spread as it did during the mid-'70s.

For which of you, desiring to build a tower, does not first sit down and count the cost, whether he has enough to complete it? Otherwise, when he has laid a foundation and is not able to finish, all who see it begin to mock him, saying, "This man began to build and was not able to finish." Or what king, going out to encounter another king in war, will not sit down first and deliberate whether he is able with ten thousand to meet him who comes against him with twenty thousand? And if not, while the other is yet a great way off, he sends a delegation and asks for terms of peace. So therefore, any one of you who does not renounce all that he has cannot be my disciple. (*Luke 14:28–33*)

When our Lord asks potential followers to "count the cost," we need to be clear this isn't an accounting or planning exercise. Uncle Murry or Merithung or their wives didn't have a clear picture of the troubles they would go through in following Jesus. "Preparing for revival" isn't like assembling building materials for a structure. It's more like the tremendous uncertainty of surrendering to the king who has more power than you do—and trusting! While we may wish for comfort and ease, those wishes can't prevail over seeking our Lord.

Ultimately, our expectancy, our hunger is something each of us can contribute to seeing Holy Spirit move in our midst. And 1 Peter 2:12 remains a command and a promise—a promise for any community, in any time period:

Keep your conduct among the Gentiles honorable, so that when they speak against you as evildoers, they may see your good deeds and glorify God on the day of visitation.

He will visit!

CHAPTER 15

The Severe Hand of God

My son, do not regard lightly the discipline of the Lord, nor be weary when reproved by Him. . . . Therefore let us be grateful for receiving a kingdom that cannot be shaken, and thus let us offer to God acceptable worship, with reverence and awe, for our God is a consuming fire. (*Hebrews 12:5, 28–29*)

Before exploring how our Lord avenges His children when they're wronged by people, let's look at Uncle Murry's account of how our Lord judged him:

In 1983, He rebuked me with a severe punishment. I lost my government engineering job from Jan. 3, 1983 until May 14, 1987. All my efforts to avert my punishment went to no effect. I realized my disobedience and sins and wept bitterly and confessed before Him.[206]

Is it possible that the intimacy of Uncle Murry's relationship with our Lord gave him freedom to see this earthly injustice as God's correction?

It's also impressive that in the Naga culture, which can be described as a shame-and-honor-based culture,[207] that Uncle Murry is open and public with his confession, distributing four thousand copies of it![208] The reader may remember Mhono saying, "Because here the culture is so different, no? Feeling shy, feeling shame, it is the main thing."

Uncle Murry's children and wife do add the earthly perspective which helps shine light on his words: he had backed his cousin running for a Nagaland political office in an election. His cousin was defeated, and the winning candidate sought vengeance on Uncle Murry and had him suspended from his government job. His eldest son Thungbemo remembers his father trying to earn money in different ways during those four years; they worked together and tried selling blankets for a time. His dad was involved in beginning some of the first coal mining in Nagaland. But none of his efforts flourished. During these four-plus years, Uncle Murry did venture out on some ministry trips:

> During this 50-month period, I traveled seven times to India[209] preaching the gospel and my faithful God followed me with signs and wonders. Many sick people, suffering from cancer, paralysis, blindness, demonic oppression, etc. received their wonderful healing from the Lord Jesus through me. Two times, Brother Toshi, Evangelist, traveled with me.[210]

It's fascinating that Toshi, the Ao evangelist, is still involved—almost four decades after he appeared in the accounts of the first wave of revival among the Lotha people! In addition, it's striking that to Uncle Murry, only leaving his job and pursuing full-time ministry counted as obedience. In a different tract, with a handwritten date of April 1994, he dates his obedience from his leaving government service in 1991:

> Prodigal Son Restored: I came back to my Father in the year 1991 after wandering many years in the barren land of sin and shame, in the life of a prodigal son. My Father received me with tender kisses

and He was relieved of His long-troubled heart by my safe return. "He restoreth my soul." (Psalm 23:3)[211]

Thankfully, in the meantime Uncle Murry had been vindicated in the world's eyes:

In May 1987 I was recalled to resume my service through the kindness of Mr. Obed, the then commissioner of the Vigilance Dept. (May God remember him and bless him.) In 1988 my punishment was fully lifted through the kindness of Mr. Chetri, the then commissioner, Works and Housing Dept., the department to which I belonged. (May God remember him and richly bless him.) Praise God I also received all 50 months of my pending pay, treating my 50 months absence from duty as regular duty.[212]

But once he was launched on his mission, Uncle Murry continued to wrestle with what he saw as God's will and his own desires. In fact, a later tract details another act of his disobedience, under the imposing title "The Wages of Sin Is Death":

The Lord directed me to set up this center in Siliguri immediately after the "Sikkim Harvest" [his initial meetings and revival training school in Namchi, Sikkim]. But because of my feeble and wavering faith, I delayed obeying the Lord's commandment till a warning came "If you do not carry on the work I commanded, I will withdraw the GIFT, the Ripened Harvest, from you as I withdrew the Holy Spirit from King Saul and gave it to David."

Now, during my hesitant days, the Lord took away my beloved sister and brother (both younger) my sister on Nov. 18, 1993; and my brother on Jan. 20, 1994 in two months time. Both of them by sudden death—heart attacks.

I wanted to be with them comfortably, so I lost terribly. I'd rather be away from them in the commandment of God so that we all live more and help each other in the service of the Lord. "I realized too late." "I obeyed after a disaster."[213]

Then on the next page he closes his tract and appeal, his thoughts continuing:

Dear brothers and sisters in Christ,

We are not living by our wisdom nor by riches and might. We are entirely in the hands of the ONE who created you and me. He is the one who controls your life.

I tried to get someone, a prophet of God, to replace me. I repeatedly tried to create excuses for myself by telling the Lord, "I am poor," "I am unlearned," "I am old…" Paul said "The gift and calling of God are irrevocable (Romans 11:29)."

Now I have learnt "To obey is better than sacrifice (1 Samuel 15:22)."

It is better to go than to send someone or money.[214]

Supernatural acts of judgment may not be mentioned in many revival histories, but were certainly part and parcel of the supernatural move of God in Nagaland. Mhono related one instance she knew of:

In Wokha, in Lotha Baptist Church, they invited Lano Longchar, this Ao man, to speak in the revival time. And he was speaking, and suddenly he called out a man's name: "Come up and you repent before God! Otherwise you're going to die very soon!"

Like that! So a man with that name was there—he was in church for the first time—just to visit only he went. He's like a tough guy, very proud, he used to drink—quite well to-do. That day only he went with friends. His friends told him—"It must be you. Go—just go and confess your sins." He said, "No, no, I'm not the only one here with that name." He just hardened his heart and went away. And the next day he was in his Jeepsy, he was picking up his car, and something happened, just went down—had an accident—and he died there, in a very easy and unexpected place.

Mhono's close friend's husband was in the car and barely escaped by leaping out. He walks with a lift in his shoe to this day because of the accident. Mhono thought this took place about 1980.

Ponder and Apply

One wonders how contemporary Christians would approach Uncle Murry's experience of being wrongly suspended from his livelihood for four years! Would we see it as our Father's loving discipline?

Enough said.

CHAPTER 16

Vengeance Is the Lord's

> Beloved, never avenge yourselves, but leave it to the wrath of God, for it is written, "Vengeance is mine, I will repay, says the Lord." (*Romans 12:19*)

> But though He may take vengeance on you for my sake, my hand will not be against you. (*1 Samuel 24:12b, REB*)

As our Naga family shared their story, they gave several instances of the Lord bringing judgment on people who had come against them. The first example Mhono gave was what happened to the young man who tried to murder Uncle Murry early in his Christian life. When her future husband was in technical college, he was brilliant, particularly at mathematics. His academic ability provoked one of his fellow students to become consumed with envy. It happened that as exams were coming, a different student, a friend of Uncle Murry's, was ill with typhoid fever. No one else was looking after the invalid, so Uncle Murry was caring for him. The young man who was filled with envy knew Murry was going to take some boiled milk up to the invalid's room, so he hid by the staircase and jumped Murry in a surprise attack. He stabbed Murry, aiming for the chest—*but the knife went just between Murry's arm and chest and didn't harm him*. Needless to say, Murry spilled the milk—and ran to his own room. But he knew he was still in danger. Uncle Murry ran away to a teacher's home and reported the attack.

When the school authority called both students in to settle the matter, Murry jumped in first and said: "I forgive him." Before the would-be murderer could say anything, Mhono said that her future husband declared, "'I forgive him in the name of Jesus and I don't hold any grudge.' He came forward and shook hands with that guy." Needless to say, the school authority was surprised, and agreed not to punish the assailant since Murry had forgiven him.

But this wasn't the end of the story—because Murry was now paralyzed with fear and couldn't study. He didn't do as well on his exams as the would-be murderer, but Murry still got a government job, as did his assailant. The India central government was pouring money into Nagaland during this time. "But, that guy, after joining the government service for not even a year, got in an accident and suffered a TERRIBLE death." His accident, like the man Lano Longchar had called out in a meeting, was in an automobile. Mhono told us this while she was with her daughter Ajano, who reminded her about another part of the story: the would-be murderer had a co-conspirator, who had been part of plotting Uncle Murry's death. "Lightning struck him. Then he was in bed for nearly two years and died. God took revenge. I think my husband visited him when he was in bed." After sharing this story, Mhono got quiet for dramatic effect to emphasize: "So from all these things I understand that my husband is chosen of God."

Another instance of what Mhono saw as God's judgment falling on someone who did them wrong related to her own healthcare. She'd had health issues as a mom and couldn't properly care for her children. "I was so weak, I suffered so much, every day, if I don't get fever in the morning, I will get fever in the evening, because of an issue in my womb." So she traveled some 240 miles from her town into the state of Assam, to the biggest city in northeast India, Guwahati:

> When I went to Guwahati for my operation, the doctor did not treat me properly, thinking that I would die. "It's already cancer, so she won't survive." They thought like that. So I wasn't given treatment properly in his hospital. So I came home. Before reaching my home, the wound from the operation became infected. And pus was formed. And when it had broken my whole skirt was soaked with pus, because they didn't give me proper treatment.

Fortunately, she had reached a city in Nagaland where her brother-in-law had a nursing facility. She was taken directly there and he treated her and told her she would have died otherwise.

The Murrys heard later from a relative in Guwahati that both the doctor's adult children had died, one from a fever his father wasn't able to treat successfully despite intense effort and the other one from drowning. "After some time, the father died, maybe because of sorrow. They are Hindu—they do not know—when you don't love God's children, but when you touch . . ." She stopped short, interrupted by a phone call, but the implication was clear—she saw God had taken vengeance on those who'd done her wrong.

There were other times our Lord intervened on behalf of this family, enforcing justice. David Murry recounted several instances besides the judgment on Uncle Murry's would-be murderer. For instance, David finished the story of what Uncle Murry saw as his discipline from the Lord when Uncle Murry was suspended from his job: "The politician who did all the harm to Dad lost the next election, money, everything—his car went underneath a truck—and he died a terrible, gruesome death." This politician had said he would make Uncle Murry "SOOOO poor, he will even sell his children."[215]

Another instance David remembered occurred during Uncle Murry's mission work. After being in Sikkim six months: "They went to Nepal to buy supplies; to get a keyboard and coats." When they came back into Sikkim, the border guard confiscated all their purchases. They had spent what little money they had. "My dad warned him, 'This is God's property. It won't be good later on.'" Sure enough, later one of the Murrys "saw in their dream" the border guard was really sick. They went back to the border post and "found out he had cancer. Dad wanted to pray for him, but within a short time he died of cancer."[216]

After being based in Sikkim for some time, Uncle Murry felt called to set up a base to the south, outside the city of Siliguri, West Bengal. Initially he was renting a place. Mhono was still working in Wokha, Nagaland, so she'd only join him during school vacations. Uncle Murry would rent a house belonging to a Hindu or a Buddhist, and the landlords would "look down on us." Partly this was because of the number and type of visitors who would come to see Uncle Murry:

> So many people would come from Nepal and Sikkim in search of him, and when they came and were with him they started shouting, praying and speaking in tongues. So the owner wouldn't be happy. He was evicted several times. After staying here and there, he started looking to buy. He checked several places but he wasn't satisfied because it wasn't according to what he saw in his dream.

Then at last he found land that matched what he'd seen in his dream: "So we purchased this land." But our Lord had to do battle on behalf of His children again to complete the purchase because *after paying for the land, the rich Hindu owner refused to give the title deed to Uncle Murry.* Uncle Murry went back to him several times. At last, Uncle Murry reached a point of frustration where he turned the matter over to the Lord. He went and told the seller, "It's now between you and the Lord—it's His property, and I won't be able to pray for you or intervene." Shortly after he did this, the seller's mother went insane. The woman had been involved in Hindu witchcraft, so that may have been a factor in the spiritual warfare. The seller handed over the papers!

Ponder and Apply

My focus has been so much on Jesus accepting those society rejects, whether tax collectors or prostitutes, that I forget that he describes judgment at times as well. While we can think His denunciations in Matthew 23 are just for people stuck in dead religion, His earlier words might apply more broadly:[217]

> Then he began to denounce the cities where most of his mighty works had been done, because they did not repent. "Woe to you, Chorazin! Woe to you, Bethsaida! For if the mighty works done in you had been done in Tyre and Sidon, they would have repented long ago in sackcloth and ashes. But I tell you, it will be more bearable on the day of judgment for Tyre and Sidon than for you. And you, Capernaum, will you be exalted to heaven? You will be brought down to Hades. For if the mighty works done in you had been done in Sodom, it would have remained until this day. But I tell you that it will be more tolerable on the day of judgment for the land of Sodom than for you." (Matthew 11:20–24)

Wow, those words are sobering. The Murry family walks in the tension of being aware that God's judgment has actually fallen on people who've done them wrong, but at the same time they're able to leave vengeance completely in our Lord's hands and refuse to rejoice at anyone's hardship.

> This is evidence of the righteous judgment of God, that you may be considered worthy of the kingdom of God, for which you are also suffering—since indeed God considers it just to repay with affliction those who afflict you. (2 Thessalonians 1:5–6)

Do not rejoice when your enemy falls,
and let not your heart be glad when he stumbles,
lest the Lord see it and be displeased,
and turn away His anger from him. (*Proverbs 24:17–18*)

Any evidence of a similar pattern in our own lives leads us to walk in awe and reverence!

When the young men came in they found her dead, and they carried her out and buried her beside her husband. And great fear came upon the whole church and upon all who heard of these things. (*Acts 5:10b–11*)

CHAPTER 17

Suffering: Soil or Fertilizer for Revival?

Since therefore Christ suffered in the flesh, arm yourselves with the same way of thinking, for whoever has suffered in the flesh has ceased from sin, so as to live for the rest of the time in the flesh no longer for human passions but for the will of God. (*1 Peter 4:1–2*)

But woe to you, O earth and sea, for the devil has come down to you in great wrath, because he knows that his time is short! (*Revelation 12:12b*)

The initial supernatural moves of the Lord started before the Indian military operations that quickly took on genocidal overtones in 1955. There must be some relationship between the ongoing suffering that came then and God's mercy being poured out in such a profound way. But what's the relationship? It doesn't appear to be clearly symmetrical or proportional. Merithung and Uncle Murry's families certainly were affected, but there were those who suffered much more. How does general suffering among a people contribute to a spiritual atmosphere that results in our Lord's blessing toward some who respond to Him?

How does one properly convey a sense of the ongoing trauma and terror that the Naga people have lived with and through, without causing a normal reader's mind to freeze up? Can we read a simple paragraph like this summary of the attacks and grasp what it means?

> The testimony of the Nagas who saw and experienced the critical period reveal that by 1955, "the military forces went on burning almost all the villages with all contents in the Naga Hills District and the villages were regrouped in a central place and confined [in] strong stockades and the inhabitants were not allowed to go out from the stockades so that the underground Naga workers were cut off from their families, communication and supplies. The church leaders were persecuted by the Indian military forces, church buildings were desecrated [and] used as rest camps for Indian forces. The inhabitants were collected in the church buildings and tortured there, girls and women were molested, raped and beaten by the Indian forces sometimes inside the church buildings."[218]

It seems possible that the entire Naga society, whether they were supporting the underground forces, simply trying to survive, or even cooperating with the Indian army, would in some way be affected with PTSD (post-traumatic stress disorder). A more detailed account of the tragedy can be found in the excellent book *From Head-Hunters to Church Planters* by Paul Hattaway.[219]

How did this ongoing struggle affect the Murry family directly? Mhono did relate a double escape she endured in 1963 some months before her wedding. As a Class 10[220] schoolgirl, she went to Kohima with her father Merithung to prepare for and then take her exams, during the time her father was translating the Bible. Her friends and classmates stayed in "a very big house" but because of the opposition to the revival, Mhono and her dad stayed in a "very small house," owned by a revivalist couple. It was Good Friday night, and she had just gone to her room to study:

> My window was just open, so I tried to close my window—as I closed my window, I heard gunshots! Tuuuuung—like that. So I was afraid! "What's that?" Then suddenly I locked the window and then suddenly—R-R-R-R—R-R-R-R—R-R-R-R everywhere! Firing! My father and family were in the kitchen, I was in the room. So my father called to me "Lie down, lie down on the floor!" So I just lie down on the floor AND the fighting became non-stop. Only at midnight the fighting stopped! The military people were just above from where the gunshots are coming. So they threw all their grenade bombs near our house! . . . But NONE of them exploded!! Ayyy—yaa. How great is our God!

Are we prepared for the evidence of revival being an escape from certain destruction? This narrow escape had already been piggybacked on another one. Mhono kept having a feeling about the previous place they had stayed, and kept asking her dad to move: "At last, he yielded to my request. 'Okay, then, let us go down to your brother Neilie's house.' because we were thinking as one family, in those days. Revivalist people—one family." The next day after they moved, the first homeowner received different guests—two people who'd just been discharged from the hospital. That night there was shooting by that house—bullets went through the thatch walls and killed both guests—in the very beds where Mhono and her father had just stayed. "So, my father came down and told me, 'Ohhh I was scolding at you, but it's the Holy Spirit that prompted you!' My father was very much surprised—like that we were saved!"

After these two near-escapes, we can imagine how hard it would be to study for exams. On top of that, she didn't know where they could stay because of the "extreme hatred" between the "revivalists and Baptists." So they moved to an old house called "Faith Home."

Why is it called "Faith Home?" Because the real revivalists, evangelists, they went out to serve the villages, preach the gospel, come back home and when they come back, they used to stay there. Take rest there. So cooks were also there. Girls who committed their lives were also there to cook for them, like that. In this house I was accommodated. And where shall I study? No place to study. I carry small purse to keep my books and small pack to keep my groceries. That's all—so I used candle and used this small basket as table. I put the candle there and I read my book there on my bed.

She didn't have the best atmosphere to study in, but nevertheless God was gracious and she passed all her exams, while her friends "who were lodged in a very good building" didn't and had to repeat several subjects. Mhono laughed with pleasure as she remembered back on this.

But it wasn't all laughter—we had a sense that Mhono had been through suffering we would never hear about. We got a glimpse of it in her eyes, after she'd just told us about this double escape. There was a pain in her voice as she said, "So many army operations—but it's okay. We don't touch—these are touching political side, nah?" Then she lowered her voice and concluded, "It's not good."

After a back-and-forth about whether the Indian army occupation had an anti-Christian aspect to it, Mhono concluded the villagers suffered "because of the politics. Not because of their faith. Yeah, if the village people don't feed them [the independence forces], they will get killed!" But of course, if a village provided any support to the independence forces, the Indian army would attack them. Because of this dilemma and suffering, Mhono said, "God sent revival to these village people to become bold-hearted and victorious during this persecution time. God is soooo kind." A comprehensive academic study of martyrs, published in 2001, did classify ten thousand of those who died in Nagaland over these years as martyrs, because they experienced "an untimely death resulting from Christian witness."[221]

His kindness endures—and so did the fighting. It gives some sense of the length of the conflict that *two decades later*, Mhono had another escape:

We were going up to Kohima while there was fighting between the underground and the Indian army. We didn't know that. We were just looking around and going slowly. Army people were running here and there. We were leisurely looking around. I thought the Army would make us stop but they didn't. Then they told me "Go quickly, go quickly!" When I looked at the roadside I saw one guy covered with a blanket—shot dead.

Her son Thungbemo, who was listening as she told the story, said they missed the shooting by two or three minutes: "We would have been right in the middle of it."[222] In the same conversation we heard about an incident *another decade after this*, which Thungbemo's wife Serena lived through. First, here's the brief account of the incident from a long list of atrocities against Nagas by the Indian military:

December 20, 1994: The 16th Maratha Light Infantry shot dead two bus drivers of the Nagaland State Transport by pumping them with over a hundred bullets at Changki junction in Mokokchung, Nagaland.

December 27, 1994: The 16th Maratha Light Infantry under the command of Major Deepak shot dead 5 civilians at Mokokchung, Nagaland. Many women were raped and molested and their clothes were stripped off and soaked in petrol [gasoline] and other chemicals for torching houses and vehicles. In the process, 6 persons were burnt alive; 48 buildings, 89 shops, 17 vehicles, 7 two-wheelers were reduced to ashes in a four-hour operation.[223]

Although from the Lotha tribe, Serena's family was living in the Ao tribe's key city of Mokokchung then, where the Ao tribe's "mother" church has several thousand members. The words tumbled out of her so quickly as she remembered what happened:

> There was big massacre by the Indian army and then there was a ceasefire—and during ceasefire time of about 3 to 4 hours many people went out to check on their missing family members and pick up mortal remains. The sight was horrifying as the armies had burned down the shops near the mother church and people hiding inside were burned alive inside the shops. Women were made to strip off their mekhelas/sarongs [clothing] and people were made to lay prostrate in the police point main road. Many were killed and assaulted and raped.

She continued, the words still coming so quickly in her distress remembering that time:

> We had a very bad Christmas! . . . bullets were flying. It's a hilly area—so those of us who lived on the top could see the fighting going on down below. Bullets would fly, we could just see them. And then they would fall on our ceiling—because our ceiling is just tin. So you'd hear it.[224]

Yet, a bad Christmas in Mokokchung didn't necessarily result in another wave of God's supernatural power. But this couple, Thungbemo and Serena, do continue to hunger for something more—and despair of any political solutions or progress because of the rampant corruption.

Ponder and Apply

- We need to abandon any desire or view that sees a season of revival as easier than our current lifestyle, "cheaper" in terms of effort or a preservative of the past. We're not suggesting one pray for unnecessary suffering to come to our family, our community, or our society. But there is evidently a suffering for righteousness' sake that Scripture speaks of that's needed for our Lord's purposes. As noted in chapter 5, "Horror Starts after Revival Begins," the apostle Paul did say, "Now I rejoice in my sufferings for your sake, and in my flesh I am filling up what is lacking in Christ's afflictions for the sake of His body, that is, the church" (Colossians 1:24).

- In another earlier chapter we noted the impossibility of fully realizing the cost we're called to pay in following our Lord—but at the same time, let's try to count the cost of our dramatic prayers! Abraham could look at his own body, "which was as good as dead," and not weaken in faith (Romans 4:19). We can consider the reality of what's around us, and what's involved—and not weaken in faith either.

- Identify with those who suffer. As a general rule, spending attention on the usual series of news items works *against* increasing love in our hearts! Living an information-saturated life means we spend our energy on superficial moments of stimulation and conflict. But if we can focus, maybe on a particular country or mission, and identify with the stories of particular people, empathy can grow in our souls: "Remember those who are in prison, as though in prison with them, and those who are mistreated, since you also are in the body" (Hebrews 13:3).

- While we are commanded to pray for our governmental leaders and to honor them, any individual calling to be involved beyond this is fraught with difficulty, as contemporary Christian political involvement, even in fully developed republics, shows. David Murry described his father as being sympathetic to the independence movement. But Uncle Murry obviously chose never to become part of it, and in fact was employed by the government service—financed by the central government in India. Merithung Mozhüi could actually appeal to one of the occupying India commanders and say he was asking Naga people to honor their authority.[225]

There appears to be a willingness on both their parts to ignore earthly injustice in the short term because of a confidence in eternal justice. We are called as believers to respect our brothers' and sisters' individual decisions in this regard—even if we disagree intensely: "let us not pass judgment on one another" (Romans 14:13).

- We also need to avoid judging our Lord and His ways in human history! "For my thoughts are not your thoughts, neither are your ways my ways, declares the Lord. For as the heavens are higher than the earth, so are my ways higher than your ways and my thoughts than your thoughts" (Isaiah 55:8–9).

CHAPTER 18

Weeds: Part of the Harvest

His disciples came to him, saying, "Explain to us the parable of the weeds of the field." He answered, "The one who sows the good seed is the Son of Man. The field is the world, and the good seed is the sons of the kingdom. The weeds are the sons of the evil one, and the enemy who sowed them is the devil. The harvest is the end of the age, and the reapers are angels. Just as the weeds are gathered and burned with fire, so will it be at the end of the age." (*Matthew 13:36–40*)

Nineveh could be seen as an outstanding example in the Bible of revival, of a massive awakening of social and spiritual change. Jonah, despite his reluctance, ended up bringing the message of the Lord in such a way that all parts of society repented:

The people of Nineveh took to heart this warning from God; they declared a public fast, and high and low alike put on sackcloth. When the news reached the king of Nineveh he rose from his throne, laid aside his robes of state, covered himself with sackcloth and sat in ashes. (*Jonah 3:5–6, REB*)

The people of Nineveh avoided judgment; God relented when they repented. Yet over some years the people of Nineveh returned to their old ways—and worse. The result? God's wrath was foretold by the prophet Nahum. His entire book explains that Nineveh's destruction was coming. The city was so utterly destroyed that there were questions whether it ever existed, until archaeologists started unearthing it in 1840.[226]

Will Nagaland follow Nineveh's path? Or is there enough revival fruit that has remained to escape judgment? In a section of his 1991 tract titled *O Nagaland—Sin City of the East*,[227] Uncle Murry raises a prophetic cry over the decadence in Naga society. Earlier in chapter 12, "Trying to Walk Godly in Babylon," we heard about some of his experiences with government corruption. But his concern was much bigger:

> In my previous printed tract, called "A NEW REVIVAL MINIS-TRY," I have mentioned the warning of the Lord ". . . that the sins of the people (the people of Nagaland) have exceeded the sins of Sodom and Gomorrah."
>
> About five years ago, a Hindu writer published an article in SUN magazine calling Dimapur "Sin City of the East." As we know Dimapur is not a town of one tribe of Nagaland. It belongs to all tribes of Nagaland. Dimapur, as a town, may be called Nagaland town. Thus when we say Dimapur, it means Nagaland. . . . In its geographical size and population, it has not reached the status of a city. But perhaps the writer was inspired by God to call it a city—the amount of sin committed is beyond the scope of a town. Brothers and sisters, what God says is true. "The sin of Nagaland exceeds the sin of Sodom and Gomorrah." The sin of a city is compressed in a smaller town. The time of its dangerous explosion is just at hand.

He goes on and blasts superficial worship and a common practice of sending children who haven't been born again for theological study! He quotes the strong words in James 5, telling the rich who've exploited others that they will suffer.[228] His denunciation of sin continues, and includes a specific example:

In December 1990 two evangelists came to Wokha from India. While coming home at 8 p.m. after attending family worship at a believer's house, a group of young men, in the street, some drunk with drugs and some with liquor, started beating and punching at the two evangelists without reason. The young evangelist, who was beaten more, remarked, "I have physically experienced the 'Sin City of the East.' Very dangerous Nagaland. Is this the kind of a Christian state?"

Uncle Murry then makes the obvious comparison to what happened to the two angels warning Lot in Sodom and Gomorrah in Genesis 19:1–13.[229] He follows his general words of warning to Nagaland, decrying particularly the sin in Dimapur, with warnings addressed at two specific groups—government and church leaders (the words in parentheses are in the original):

"Hear this, ye *heads of the House of Jacob*[230] (heads of each tribe of Nagaland) and *princes* (ministers)[231] of the house of *Israel* (Nagaland), that *abhor judgment* (fear to do good and justice) and *pervert equity* (turn the law upside down).

"They build *Zion* (the assembly house) with blood, and *Jerusalem* (Kohima)[232] with iniquity.

"The heads thereof *judge for reward* (do their duty for bribes) and the *priests* (heads of the Church) thereof teach for hire and the *prophets* (professing themselves as God's agents but practicing devil's devices for their benefits) thereby divine for money; yet will they lean upon the Lord, and say, "Is not the Lord upon us? No evil can come upon us. Therefore shall *Zion* (Assembly house) for your sake be plowed as a field and *Jerusalem* (Kohima) shall become heaps, and *the mountains of the house* (beautiful church buildings in the lovely towns and villages upon the hills) as the *high places* (Satanic sanctuaries) of the forest." (*Micah 3:9–12, KJV*)[233]

We may have heard similar warnings. Still, the fire in Uncle Murry's words is so strong that we may want to look for asbestos gloves before reading further! He goes on to indict the politicians' spiritual practices:

You have brought in idolatrous practices, by bringing in the ashes of cremated Hindu politicians, thus defiling the sanctity of God's children, and wearing Hindu traditional ropes and paints and introducing Hindu politicians' picture-worship.[234]

Uncle Murry's denunciation of politicians sees things in strictly black-and-white terms. It's useful as a word of balance to note that one political leader from this era, who went on to become the Chief Minister (governor, in U.S. terms) is commended in the biography of the Naga missionary Thino Peseyie for contributing 300,000 rupees for the construction of a church building in the mission field of Sikkim.[235] How many politicians are publicly known as significant supporters of cross-cultural missions?

Uncle Murry spent twice as many words on church leaders as he did on the politicians. Because of Nagaland's strategic position in the center of Southeast Asia,

God wanted to make us a Gideon's army against the army of Lucifer around us. That is why He sends revival again and again on Nagaland since 1952. But every time revival breaks out, our church leaders stand against it, and the power of the Holy Spirit movement is quenched. Brilliant students who are uncommitted to Christ are sent for theological studies, and they are used as weapons against revival.[236]

After telling about these leaders' opposition to the baptism in the Holy Spirit and the lack of signs and wonders following their preaching, Uncle Murry lists four evils the church leaders have committed:

- You are a stumbling block to Holy Spirit. (You are responsible for the death of revival. He will ask the blood of your people.)

- You have followed the doctrine of Nimrod. (God will bring the rod of Babel and smite you.)

- You have followed the path of money and power. (He will bring the Egyptian diseases upon you.)

- You have inclined to the wisdom of men, not of Him. (He will bring foolishness upon you.)[237]

He expands on this for another page, and interestingly in light of the COVID-19 pandemic, one of the things he says is: "Remember I am coming with the rod of Babel and with diseases which your own wisdom cannot heal."

Uncle Murry had endured much in government and church work, which brought him to his fiery prophecies. How much of his intensity came from disappointments and despair over his own family situation? The weeds were more than the harvest among his own children for years at a time. One of his sons, Alan, was open about the struggles Uncle Murry had to endure even into the 1990s:

Alan: And we became a little bit rebellious also.

Interviewer: So tell me about that. . . . Thungbemo introduced you to drugs. He said that he regrets that but he said that he did.

Alan: Of course we used to play music together and I used to do whatever he does. We used to go out, sneak out at night, after everybody was asleep and then go and jam with our friends—all night. Their parents just allowed them to do whatever they wanted. We used to go and jam, yeah, all night, we used to do all sorts of dreadful stuff—we were influenced so much by rock and roll. Even in a small place like Wokha, people were so much influenced by American rock and roll, British hard rock. We heard—it may not be real—but stories about those artists and we thought their lifestyle is like that. We got influenced so much by those things—drinking, smoking, and then afterwards, getting into drugs.

After discussing details of his drug abuse, and how his brother Thungbemo stopped once he got married at age 24, Alan said: "I kept on going for quite a long time, even after he stopped." He would stop and then start using again, even while his father had launched his mission work. "When I was clean, when I was out of drugs and drinking, I used to come sometimes with him and stayed with him for some time. I went to Sikkim with him for three months." Then he was clean 1996–98 while he was with Youth with a Mission (YWAM) in south India.[238] Alan is now married and clean, but still recovering from the effects of the years of drug abuse. Later on, his life experience was the reason he could expose a con artist who for several months had been scamming Uncle Murry and the ministry in Siliguri.

The Murry family experience is certainly not unique—either in their culture, or in the West. But Mhono adds her view of the other "weeds" that grew up in the Naga society—at the same time as or after the revivals:

Mhono: I will tell you why our Naga revival died down. Our Naga people were deceived by the easy money and then, alcohol. Central government sent easy money. People who went to military and got pension and then came back—they supplied them drugs and beer. In this way, Nagaland became so drunkard. And then easy money. When easy money was sent, students didn't like to study hard. I was teaching in the school. I recognized it. All they do is try to cheat! And if I'm strict with them, then they will kill me. I was threatened two or three times in the school.

Ajano: In the eighties also there was revival. But it became man-made.

Mhono: Yeah, like that. So revival died down. Laziness. Easy money. Drink. So because of all this, easy money—"I want to buy new shoes, good shoes, I want to buy new dress, I want to buy make-up, I want to construct a big house, I want to buy car." People became so worldly. And honesty was COMPLETELY crushed down, suppressed, there was no, no honesty. There was no truthfulness. There was no love of one another. Moreover, because of the independence movement, different kinds of factions came out, and then gangsters, killing people, robbing their wealth, all these kinds of evil things grew up in Nagaland.

Ajano: Addiction.

Mhono: All these affected spiritual life—so many factors are there in Nagaland. You cannot give only one or two factors. SOOOOO many factors. Like a tsunami—sin was like that. And in this way spiritual activities were completely crushed.

Mhono explained that if someone received a contract to build something, they would expect to keep at least half of the money strictly for themselves: "They think as if it is their own money, not government money." The couple's oldest daughter encountered similar corruption in hospital administration. She was on track to be put in charge, but resigned because of the corruption she encountered: "She is facing lot of financial difficulties now—but she is not regretting her decision. Anybody who can withstand all this temptation; they are chosen of God!"

Mhono went on to explain that there are problems in the church world as well. Some pastors are chosen based on family loyalty. Many pastors don't encourage people to study or to share about the Bible with others: "So not hearing from other people and not reading ourself also, how can we grow in the Spirit? Because we are lacking the spiritual food. . . .

In this way the spiritual atmosphere has completely died down here. But we should not be discouraged because there is some remnant who calls upon Jesus."

Lest we think this dim view of the Naga church and social conditions is just one family's "little bit extreme" view, let's hear from revivalist Wabang Longchari in a 2019 message to his people: "My dear fellow Nagas, today our land is in such a pathetic condition, with rampant corruption, disunity, lack of good covenants, lack of upright leaders, both political and spiritual, no development and no political solutions."[239] You'll notice he's critical of the spiritual leaders along with the political—like Uncle Murry was.

Ponder and Apply

When Jesus shared the parable of the weeds (before He explained it to His disciples in private) he closed with these words:

> And the servants of the master of the house came and said to him, "Master, did you not sow good seed in your field? How then does it have weeds?" He said to them, "An enemy has done this." So the servants said to him, "Then do you want us to go and gather them?" But he said, "No, lest in gathering the weeds you root up the wheat along with them. Let both grow together until the harvest, and at harvest time I will tell the reapers, 'Gather the weeds first and bind them in bundles to be burned, but gather the wheat into my barn.'" (Matthew 13:27–30)

Just because the fruit of Holy Spirit's work is uneven, it doesn't invalidate it. Our posture can be that of the master of the house—let the reapers make the judgment what are weeds and what is grain when the harvest is mature!

Let us deal with the weeds in our lives: our immediate surroundings! This is a large matter, and needs to be addressed in more than one spiritual arena. Still, one key one to focus on is the discipline of continuing to hear our Lord's fresh voice in prayer and reading the Bible. It's striking that Mhono can relate how people stop reading the Word because it's dry—or in their setting, because they've been told in some way that they can't understand it, that only trained leaders should teach it! I have seen some well-meaning Bible teaching send this same diabolical message in our setting—sometimes subtly, sometimes directly. We need to continually affirm Holy Spirit's ability to teach each of us everything we need to know (John 16:13). At the same time, in our connections with other believers, do we focus on applying the Word—on acting on what we've heard (2 Peter 1:8)? A focus on "what do we do with the word we've heard" brings excitement and vitality to reading the Scriptures.

CHAPTER 19

How Does Abundant Life Work?

I came that they may have life and have it abundantly. (*John 10:10b*)

If anyone would come after me, let him deny himself and take up his cross daily and follow me. For whoever would save his life will lose it, but whoever loses his life for my sake will save it. (*Luke 9:23–24*)

We can grasp the paradox of self-denial and abundant life by looking at Jesus. He must have lived the type of life He was bringing—of both dying to self and abundance.

Abundance doesn't refer just to the physical and material side of life, but that's included and where we'll start. After seeing the financial hardship that our family went through in chapter 8, "Families Pay a Price for Revival," let's look at how they did over the longer term. Mhono spoke at length about her mother, Yanasali Mozhüi:

She worked very hard. She had a very strong faith. Whenever she wanted to give help, give some gift to anyone, she would say, "Don't let other people know." She used to give like that. This way, God prospered her. When my father became old and came back from active ministry God prospered them soooo much!

Mhono said because of her mother's work, her father was able to establish Christian Model High School in Wokha in 1972 when he was 61 years old and could no longer travel in ministry. This may not seem like a route to financial provision in the West, but private schools in India often support their proprietors well.

Every morning he would go to the school and pray for the children. So many theologians, many doctors, many engineers, have come out of this school. I taught in my father's school also. One child he suffered from epilepsy, and he fell like this *(Mhono demonstrated a seizure)*, foaming. My father was very tall and very big, very strong, so my father would pick up the child, pray for him, and then he would become all right and go to class. He did his ministry in the school like that. When my father was alive even the Naga government recognized the school. They sent 27 computers.

The enrollment grew to 1,550 students, Nursery through Class 10, so Mhono's mother "kept on building, and building, and building, so there would be enough rooms for so many students. And so many teachers were employed." Eventually Merithung's health got to the point he had to use a wheelchair and couldn't be active in running the school. His death in 2006 led to a decline in the school, but up to then it had provided well for Mhono's family of origin and helped in a major way with the Murrys' ministry campaigns.

Mhono saw the same mercy and provision in her family of marriage as well. She said Uncle Murry launched out in ministry with some irregular support from several longtime friends. So in order to keep going he used the money he initially got from his pension benefits, and money from selling their land (not including the land their home was on) to put into their work. Mhono said:

> We didn't know anything and we weren't trained up properly, so we might have committed mistakes and errors in the service of God, but God is so gracious! Yes, even though he [Uncle Murry] has suffered like this, still—he's alive and we are enjoying his pension money. I'm so thankful to God—my pension money is so little! But his pension money is double mine. God is so patient to make us enjoy his pension money for a LONG time! He retired in 1990— how many years is that? Almost 30 years. NOBODY enjoys pension money so long! When I remember these things, how good is God! When I was working I could not save even a single pai[240] because I used to spend all the money, here and here, and here, like that.

> *Ajano:* Of course she was supporting Dad, also.

> *Mhono:* And our house was almost falling down—but now I consider myself to be a very rich woman. And God is supplying all of our needs—more than sufficient. And whatever I touch God is prospering me!

Of course abundance isn't just a matter of physical necessities, but most of all relationships, particularly family relationships. Like many Naga families they have been through a painful and deep valley of seeing children go completely astray, off their moorings; we've seen some of this in previous chapters. Ajano's path was a complicated story. She had a child with a man but he wouldn't commit to her—she would leave him and then return: "She was coming to us—going back again. . . . Ahhh—she suffered so much! Our relationship with Ajano was good—because she is our child." She had two more children with the man, but he never repented of "taking other girls, drinking, taking drugs" so finally the relationship ended.

Mhono related how after the final breakup, of course Ajano was crying and depressed; in large part because she had to leave the children. Their relationship had never been official, and in Nagaland, the father of the children has priority rights. Uncle Murry told Ajano to leave the children in the hands of God and pursue Him, predicting, "One day they will call you: 'Come, take the children, Ajano. We cannot make them good people.'" Mhono said her husband's words were a "real prophecy." Ajano went ahead and set out for YWAM and tried to find solace in the Lord. After a few years the children's grandfather called: "Ajano, take the children with you. From this house they will never become good persons." (The grandfather in these situations has the right to do this.) So Ajano took custody of all three of her children and took them to Siliguri as she worked with Uncle Murry there.

Even in the midst of his own family struggles Uncle Murry was still loving others in the most practical of ways. He actually adopted a child from Bhutan during his missionary days. It gives some idea of the family dynamics that he did this without consulting Mhono, who was some four hundred miles away in Nagaland. A needy mother in Bhutan approached him and he agreed to take her 10-year-old daughter. Mhono remembers that when Mary joined the family, "David was quite young at that time, around 20, something like that."

Needless to say, this development wasn't trouble-free. After much effort Mary didn't pass her class-12 exams. Her words were, "I am fed up with studying." The stress of figuring out her adopted daughter's future was taking a toll on Mhono. She described it as "mental torture—if I don't arrange any future for Mary, how can I leave her like this? Staying at home all the time may create a lot of problems, quarreling, there may not be peace at all in the house. I prayed and prayed and prayed and prayed: 'Oh God, what shall I do with this girl?'"

Mhono came up with a plan and Mary agreed. She was sent to help Ajano with the school Ajano had started as part of the ministry in Siliguri. Mary and a man working in the ministry became interested in each other, "So we gave her in marriage—God is arranging everything for us. We cannot—even if we want a very good thing, we cannot do it on our own." Mhono said, with eyes of fondness, "She's so good to me now—she understands me now, how much I loved her."

After hearing how in the heyday of the move of God Mhono's life was hell, it seemed reasonable to ask about happy memories. This eventually got us back to what the abundant life has to be based on. After remembering her times of sadness, Mhono said:

> Sometimes when I remember the word of God, I'm joyful! Sometimes when I forget the word of God, I become very tired. Sometimes I feel very alone. And I feel very discouraged also, but when I remember the word of God I am encouraged. I know, I know God has something good for me up there, that is my encouragement."

Ponder and Apply

We can't separate the abundant life Jesus brings from Himself—the gift can't be separated from the giver. Trouble and lack aren't indications we're out of sync with our Lord—and we can also be assured they're only seasons. We are the bride of Christ, and eventually we will say with the bride in Song of Songs:

> My beloved speaks and says to me:
>
> "Arise, my love, my beautiful one, and come away, for behold, the winter is past; the rain is over and gone.
>
> The flowers appear on the earth, the time of singing has come, and the voice of the turtledove is heard in our land." (*Song of Songs 2:10–12*)

May we each have grace to encourage ourselves in Him, in His word, to pass through discouragement and hard times without bitterness. His comfort is available—and we can pass it on:

> Blessed be the God and Father of our Lord Jesus Christ, the Father of mercies and God of all comfort, who comforts us in all our affliction, so that we may be able to comfort those who are in any affliction, with the comfort with which we ourselves are comforted by God. (*1 Corinthians 1:3–4*)

CHAPTER 20

Revival and Division

But others said, "How can a man who is a sinner do such signs?" And there was division among them. (*John 9:16b*)

The division spawned by our Lord's supernatural work is evidently inevitable. Some examples have been mentioned earlier. It doesn't help to turn our heads and ignore the problem—we need to study the division, in hopes of responding rightly ourselves. One story Mhono gave of her father Merithung's encounters with division started right after his conversion:

> Day and night, he read the Bible. He read in English, and then he read in Lotha, our dialect. Then he started crying and crying and crying. Why did he cry? Because in English it is so good but in Lotha, translation is not good. So how can people read the Bible and understand the word of God if the translation is like this? Then he started thinking to translate the Bible.

197

At this point she pointed to a printed Lotha Bible—her father's translation. But in a way that translation is also a memorial to division, as initially he'd started the work in a mission center opposed to the work of the Holy Spirit. Even though he volunteered and constructed a house for himself, eventually he was forced out of it. He finished the translation at home and eventually got the Assemblies of God to sponsor the printing of his translation.

> Then, some people who are against him, they reported to the administrative officer here in Wokha, and my father was arrested and put in jail. My father stayed in the jail two times. A certain day was fixed and the case was judged. The magistrate asked him, "Why did you print the Bible on your own without getting permission first?"

Merithung explained he'd gotten approval from the Assemblies of God Missions, and once that was explained the magistrate turned on his accusers and rebuked them for making a false accusation. The case was dismissed and Merithung was released.

Earlier we quoted Mhono's words that there was "extreme hatred" between those who she labeled as the Baptists and the revivalists. In our human longing for heroes we can admire, I naturally hope the hatred went only one direction—surely one "side" in such divisions walks godly and maintains love in Christ! Thankfully, this appears to be true at least in Merithung's case. Here's how Merithung responded in love when some leaders tried to use the occupying Indian army against him:

> Even if he is arrested my father could not keep quiet. So one day he went to the village of Longidang, to preach revival message there: "Repent. Come closer to God. Be filled with the Holy Spirit. Without the Holy Spirit we cannot go to heaven.". . . because in those days people do not know who is Holy Spirit.

A village leader and a pastor who opposed the revival message told the Indian army that Merithung was coming to the village to denounce the Indian government:

The military officer thought it was true, and my father was arrested. He was kept in a dungeon. And then the trial date came, he was let out of jail and he was questioned. That military guy asked him: "Merithung, what are you preaching to the people? Tell me exactly what you are preaching." So my father had to answer him. "Sir—I am preaching to the people not to kill, not to quarrel. I am preaching to the people to obey their government. I am preaching to the people, peace, the Bible, what Jesus taught us, to love one another, not to fight, not to kill, to maintain peace among their brethren. I preach to the people the teaching of Jesus Christ," my father replied. Then, the military officer said, "Ahh like that! Then we are same! We are the same." They are Hindu but they also preach about peace. "Then you and I are of the same party!" Then he called the accusers and asked them, "Tell me exactly what did Merithung preach?" They could not answer. The pastor of the village and then the panchayat[241] of the village—these two leaders were accusing my father. They could not answer. Then the military guy got angry! "Why you are bearing false report?" Then with a real big stick the military people use he wanted to smite them. But my father said, "Sir, please, please don't touch them. I forgive them. Please don't touch them." So he went out, obeying my father's request! .

The Okotso Baptist Church history tells about the divisions from their perspective. Pastor Phandeo, the pastor who welcomed Rikum's teaching, also dealt with division:

From the beginning of 1941 he served as full-time pastor as well as a teacher in the Mission School. As a true leader, he not only taught the people but set exemplary way of living, through which his church was transformed in all spheres. A mighty revival swept through Nagaland during his pastorship, but through wrong teachings and emotions of few people, many were led astray, but this strong man in the Lord stood firm in the word of God and saved his church from disintegration.[242]

A page later, the history gives more details of the division, as part of the booklet's conclusion:

During the time [1950s] some false teachers from outside Nagaland came . . . and misled the people whose faith is founded on emotions. They were taught about second baptism, without which their faith is in vain.[243] Thus, those who accepted the false teachings began to separate themselves away from the mainstream and started separate fellowship. In due course, some of these groups became the members of the Assemblies of God churches. With the passage of time, these groups split up into manifold sects, making certain villages to ring several church bells on Sunday. Some of the split away group later realized their wrong steps and rejoined the churches once left, and re-affirmed their commitment to God.[244]

Interestingly, from this description of division, the booklet goes right into a closing statement:

We are grateful to the Almighty God, who led the church of Okotso, through thick and thin, through suffering and shame all throughout these hundred years and has enabled us to enter the second Jubilee on December 27–29, 2004. Let it be known throughout generations together to come, that the sufferings and humiliations suffered by our forefathers, are never never in vain, but, "Looking unto Jesus, the Author and Finisher of our faith," we will continue to toil and overcome until He comes.[245]

The divisions resulting from God's supernatural work are so sad from both heaven and earth's perspective, yet some sound almost like a parody. For a number of years, Merithung pastored and led a church in Wokha which his daughter and son-in-law didn't join, despite their common revival interest. Ajano described how Uncle Murry was even rejected by their "Holy Spirit" church: "He was talking about the Holy Spirit and one man from the audience shouted at him, 'Ohh, stop, stop, stop—enough! Don't talk about these things' in front of everyone! I was so embarrassed." Her father's response was to stop talking and leave the platform. And interestingly, in light of the earlier chapter on God's vengeance, the shouter became "a little crazy" and then died.

Ajano's brother David gave the history on why his father and his grandfather ended up in separate congregations. At a statewide level, what had been one group became two: the Nagaland Christian Revival Church and Christian Revival Church. Then a third came into being, as the Assemblies of God were invited in. So what did this mean for Uncle Murry's family?

> We were first at Assemblies of God church, this little church and then there was a church split. By default we became A-G 1 because they called themselves A-G 2. By that time the Baptists thought that the A-G and what they called "the revival people," were crazy. And so, we [the children] felt ashamed to go to this small church—because the Baptist church was huge and majestic! And here we are in this little itty-bitty church [building]. We felt ashamed—my parents didn't. But my parents also definitely felt the persecution. What happened was that again, for whatever reason, the church again became Christian Revival Church—I don't know how that happened. Later on we were just coasting along as CRC, and then suddenly the Jesus Only group comes in and the majority—by that time my grandfather had started his own CRC church. My dad did not go with my grandfather when they left. Our family stayed back. Then when the Jesus Only group came in that was the last straw.

We didn't have a church! Dad didn't know where to go; because there were some fundamental issues he didn't agree with my grandfather's church, some of the doctrinal practices, some of the things they would do. One of the things my dad, and even my mom, didn't agree with grandfather's brand of doctrine was—before they would start a service; they would read Ephesians, chapter 6, and they would cast out the devil. At the first of every service, no matter what. These are some of the extremes that came about because of the lack of teaching. And that my grandfather carried on. My mom and dad said "You don't have to do that, you can just start praising God and darkness will flee."[246]

Ponder and Apply

I do not ask for these only, but also for those who will believe in me through their word, that they may all be one, just as you, Father, are in me, and I in you, that they also may be in us, so that the world may believe that you have sent me. The glory that you have given me I have given to them, that they may be one even as we are one, I in them and you in me, that they may become perfectly one, so that the world may know that you sent me and loved them even as you loved me. (*John 17:20–23*)

Our Lord's words need to be viewed in conjunction with His apostle's later observation, when Paul wrote to the immature believers in Corinth:

For, in the first place, when you come together as a church, I hear that there are divisions among you. And I believe it in part, for there must be factions among you in order that those who are genuine among you may be recognized. (*1 Corinthians 11:18–19*)

One way Paul's words can be read is that there is a place in God's economy for division—to see how we respond to it! Do we keep loving as He does? The general operating principle for many approaching the question of Christian unity has been summed up in these words: "If we preserve unity in essentials, liberty in nonessentials, and charity in both, our affairs will be in the best position."[247] Of course, then the question still remains: What are essentials? For instance, believers touched by the Spirit among the Naga tribes believed repentance for salvation was needed before any act of water baptism. That led to division and separation from those who didn't see the faith that way.

As importantly, how is unity to be expressed? Unity of a husband and wife, or within a family, is a critical starting point. The ability of Merithung to remain committed to his son-in-law's mission, even though they hadn't been part of the same church body for years, is impressive.

Can we picture unity happening while there are still human organizations and structures, with all the motivations (and temptations) those bring to our lives? We can agree with statements, or principles, and not be connected at a heart level. We do know that harmony in music doesn't involve everyone singing the same note, but in the notes blending together. Unity isn't uniformity.

It's easy to counsel humility and respect, particularly in our spiritual interchanges and conversations—yet both our Lord and Paul were unsparing, even contemptuous, of some who perverted the faith, or God's ways. But given that we may not have their level of discernment of people's hearts, or what constitutes legalism or Pharisaism, it seems wise to walk cautiously in attacking other professing believers.

Let's exercise change with our imaginations: Can we form a mental picture of "more" unity in our immediate spiritual surroundings? It may be within our immediate family, small group, or church body—or workplace or school. What would more unity and harmony look like there?

From there, can we take a step outside our own comfort zones—across whatever divide may exist within the body of Christ in our immediate surroundings? We don't need to solve history—we need to respond to Holy Spirit's nudges where we are.

CHAPTER 21

Where Does New Wine Fit?

And no one pours new wine into old wineskins. Otherwise,
the new wine will burst the skins; the wine will run out and
the wineskins will be ruined. No, new wine must be poured
into new wineskins. And no one after drinking old wine wants
the new, for they say, "The old is better." (*Luke 5:37–39*)

J esus's words are an interesting addition and contrast to His prayer for
unity quoted in the previous chapter. His words answer a question about
a difference between His followers and the followers of John the Baptist and
the Pharisees. They're a vivid picture of the challenge new spiritual movements face. There's an unwillingness on the part of many to embrace "new
wine"—the old tastes better. And if people try to put the new wine into old
traditions, old structures—it doesn't work.

The formation of "revivalist" churches in Nagaland is certainly an example of both these patterns. But these weren't the only new wineskins birthed
from this move of the Holy Spirit. There are other structures, beyond

church bodies, where the common life of Christ is lived out. We see three basic forms in Acts 19 and 20:

> And he [Paul] entered the synagogue and for three months spoke boldly, reasoning and persuading them about the kingdom of God. But when some became stubborn and continued in unbelief, speaking evil of the Way before the congregation, he withdrew from them and took the disciples with him, reasoning daily in the hall of Tyrannus. This continued for two years, so that all the residents of Asia heard the word of the Lord, both Jews and Greeks. . . .
>
> Sopater the Berean, son of Pyrrhus, accompanied him; and of the Thessalonians, Aristarchus and Secundus; and Gaius of Derbe, and Timothy; and the Asians, Tychicus and Trophimus. These went on ahead and were waiting for us at Troas, but we sailed away from Philippi after the days of Unleavened Bread, and in five days we came to them at Troas, where we stayed for seven days. From Miletus, Paul sent to Ephesus for the elders of the church. (*Acts 19:8–10; 20:4–6, 17*)

The first structure is Paul's class in the synagogue, and then the hall of Tyrannus. It is a time-limited training class or organization. Eventually these training classes may become an ongoing structure—a school, college, university—but still with the common characteristic that students in the community, in the structure, are only there for a period of time and plan to move on. Then we see a second structure—the team of workers Paul had assembled. This can be termed a missionary team or society. Believers who have joined together on a common mission, and have made some degree of commitment to one another, make up such a team or society.[248] The time period may or may not be defined, the degree of commitment may vary— but there's a commitment to particular people and a purpose beyond simply following Christ in a general way. When this is done in a comprehensive way in a single location, we can have a commune or a monastery. The third community is a church—a gathering of believers, in a locale.[249] These three ways of living out our common life in Christ may not exhaust all the possibilities, but they help us think through how believers are living out our common life.

We can see, by looking at Paul's reference from the book of Philippians, a fourth arrangement: a network of supporters, senders, partners:

> And you Philippians yourselves know that in the beginning of the gospel, when I left Macedonia, no church entered into partnership with me in giving and receiving, except you only. Even in Thessalonica you sent me help for my needs once and again. . . . I am well supplied, having received from Epaphroditus the gifts you sent, a fragrant offering, a sacrifice acceptable and pleasing to God. (*Philippians 4:15–16, 18*)

Sender networks are often fluid and less defined, but still a critical way of living out our common life as believers. We can see the people immediately involved in most parachurch ministries fit the category of a mission team or society. In turn, such ministries will often have a network of supporters, who help and pray for the particular mission of the ministry. Christian schools, at whatever level, can be seen as training centers. And a group gathering in a home or a building, welcoming others to gather with them, is a church.

Yet, inevitably in the actual life of an organization or community, we see some aspect of all three—church gatherings have temporary training classes; colleges ask for a behavior commitment (like a team would); mission teams end up providing the love and family life of a local church.

Looking at the Murry and Mozhüi family history, one can see how their personal revival experiences developed and were eventually lived out in new community, new organizational structures. One part of this development became new church gatherings, and then a whole network of churches, and eventually three denominations.[250]

The family embraced new wineskins. In fact, a key moment of Uncle Murry's life came as he sought direction—at a prayer center:

> I decided to go down to Chathe[251] where a prayer center was open. I went there fasting.[252] . . . During that time it became a sweet place and I came out. . . . And our pastor[253] also encouraged me. . . . that I had to go and start the revival. So I went down to Dimapur, to find somebody who could take me. . . . One boy from Sikkim, Himalayan region . . . I asked if he was going again or not. He said he was going. . . . So I followed him to reach out in Sikkim, Namchi, his village.[254]

The family has used prayer centers as a wineskin to seek the Lord for direction. The revival they'd experienced was also eventually expressed in other structures. We've told how Merithung and his wife founded an elementary and secondary school, Christian Model High School, in Wokha in 1972. Eventually, Uncle Murry would start a "ministry." He describes being directed by the Holy Spirit to set up this new wineskin, "a prayer and praise center in the city of Siliguri, as forerunner of the coming mighty . . . explosion of Holy Spirit Revival." He gives three purposes for the ministry:

i.   Wait for the promise of the coming Latter Rain revival through fasting and prayer.

ii. To conduct short term revival campaign trainings to the young people of Nepal, Sikkim, Bhutan, and Darjeeling district.[255]

iii. To campaign for revival to the whole region (Four corner courts).[256]

A prayer and praise center is a ministry with a particular purpose, like a mission team—and it provided training to others, as this was part of Uncle Murry's purpose. The revival in Nagaland had already spawned many prayer centers, as the activity schedule or life of a local church didn't provide enough room to express the life of God spawned by the revival.

Nagaland Christian Revival Church tells in their history about this development, with a brief allusion to how the original Christian Revival Church split in two:

> Tossed with the other denominational waves resulting in the split of the NCRC, the leaders felt the need of the Holy Spirit's leading more than before. They devoted more time in prayer seeking God's will and guidance for the church. Some dedicated their lives to full time prayer ministry by setting up Prayer Centers. . . . Many of them left their own churches and places and dedicated themselves to prayer full time. Prayer meetings were conducted almost every weekend which exerted a tremendous impact upon the churches—vitalizing spiritual fervor in the churches. Fasting and prayer with various revelations through visions and prophecies were the order of the meetings. Conventions, crusades and Bible classes were replaced by such meetings.[257]

The account rolls right into the problems this development created:

Manifestations of the gifts of the Holy Spirit in various forms were in abundance and [believers were] giving less importance to the Word of God. The prayer warriors were mostly elderly people with less education. There was a seeming gap in between the educated younger generation and the elderly prayer warriors. The elderly prayer warriors considered the young educated ones as to be more intellectual but less spiritual, preoccupied with theological and doctrinal issues, denominational and organizational problems. They were impressed by Paul's writing that "Letter kills but Spirit gives life." Whereas the young educated leaders viewed the elders with respect but . . . in need of Biblical guidance. They held onto "Believe not every spirit. Let it be judged . . . rightly dividing the word of truth." There was an unexpressed feeling of two parallel leadership within the NCRC viz: Prayer warriors who gave more priority to prayer centers and theologians whose priority was to run theological colleges as their ministry. A danger of inner dispute and division was easily averted because of the undisputed leadership of the pioneer revival leaders. The unity of the pioneer leaders, their dedication to ministry and commitment to the church could hold the NCRC together.[258]

The booklet said that at that time there were twenty-seven prayer centers and eleven theological colleges under the denomination! The new wine has certainly found, or formed, new wineskins. A page later, the booklet reported on the prayer centers and theological colleges which had been going, at that point, *for more than twenty-five years already:*

Chathe Prayer Center: This Prayer Center is called House of Prayer for All People, established in 1965. Rev. Delievi was the founder of this center with all dedication he devoted his whole life unmarried to the prayer ministry. The center is looked after by the five churches around Chathe. This is the largest Prayer Center having hundreds of inmates, having 23 full time prayer warriors.[259]

Pughoboto Prayer Center: It was established in 1978. Presently there are four full-time prayer warriors at the center. Initially this prayer center was established at Ghathashi in 1971, and then shifted to Mishilimi in 1973. Later on it was permanently established in Pughoboto Town on land donated by Rev. Vitokhu.[260]

The booklet went on to describe three more prayer centers, each of which had been going for more than twenty-five years. The description of the prayer center in Kigwema mentions that Mrs. Tuothsenuo had been a full-time prayer warrior there since 1978, and as of 2012 was 83 years old:

A Prayer House is attached to almost all the Christian Revival Churches with full time prayer warriors. Prayer Centers are established in many places before any church is planted in many mission fields. . . .[to open the door for] those who seek the Lord with miracles of healing and getting answers to various spiritual problems and needs.[261]

In any context, this last area can lead to problems, as people come to the prayer centers and the flesh gets mixed in with the Spirit. I have heard several examples of people receiving bad advice in a prayer center. At the same time, someone familiar with both the overall sweep of church history and the starting of monasteries—or even recent events like the "Jesus movement," primarily in California during the early 1970s, with its Christian communes—can see the parallels. Holy Spirit is inspiring people to express more devotion, or to express it in different ways than the conventional local gathering provides.

Ponder and Apply

Some readers may be part of what we've heard called the "done" group—that you're "done with church" as you know it! Others may just be uncomfortable with a sense that their current church or ministry life doesn't really match all we see in the Bible. No doubt all of us, at some level, are looking for something more. The tension we live in is summed up by these questions:

- What's the essence of church? Or what's the minimum we need to "have church"?
- What's the most we can have? What will God allow us to walk in, this side of heaven?[262]

Let's keep stretching—and resist the dynamic our Lord spoke of: "And no one after drinking old wine wants the new, for they say, 'The old is better'" (Luke 5:39). May we be ready to try new expressions, new ways of meeting, and consider whether what we are called to next may be training, no matter what our age. Or, we can make some type of commitment to live out at least an aspect of our Christian life with others who have a particular focus, whether it be helping the needy where we are, caring for the preborn, or sending harvesters into other cultures. Allow me to adapt something Australian Bible teacher Kevin Connor (among others) has said: when we have only the written Word, we dry up; only the Spirit, we blow up; only fellowship, we don't look up—but with all three, we *grow* up.

CHAPTER 22

Too Different, Too Big, or Too Mundane?

Now to Him who is able to do far more abundantly than all that we ask or think, according to the power at work within us, to Him be glory in the church and in Christ Jesus throughout all generations, forever and ever. Amen. (*Ephesians 3:20–21*)

Behold, I am doing a new thing; now it springs forth, do you not perceive it?

I will make a way in the wilderness and rivers in the desert.

The wild beasts will honor me, the jackals and the ostriches,

for I give water in the wilderness, rivers in the desert, to give drink to my chosen people. (*Isaiah 43:19–20*)

The work of the Holy Spirit among the Naga people has been so massive numerically, and so extreme in some of its manifestations, that we can be tempted to ignore it. It can be hard to imagine in a Western church context. The responses of people like Merithung and Uncle Murry can be seen as "a little bit extreme"—or too different from our experience to see how we can emulate them. Yet, if nothing else, the sheer statistics should inspire us.

At the same time, parts of this revival history can be so mundane—a missionary-minded headmaster cries over Merithung's soul, to no effect—until years later. Thino is seeking God as a young man, hears Billy Graham preach—and then four years later gets born again. Family problems and church conflict occur that may surpass anything we've experienced. Yet these were all part of a movement that culminates in census statistics that can't be ignored!

There are many who are expecting a great harvest—and great turning to our Lord as we approach the return of Christ. But what's the biblical basis for this expectancy?

There are two key passages that make clear there will be a great harvest—and a couple of parables that hint at it. Let's start reading at the end of the parable known as "the wheat and the tares (or weeds)" from Matthew 13:30–33:

> Let both grow together until the harvest, and at harvest time I will tell the reapers, "Gather the weeds first and bind them in bundles to be burned, but gather the wheat into my barn." He put another parable before them, saying, "The kingdom of heaven is like a grain of mustard seed that a man took and sowed in his field. It is the smallest of all seeds, but when it has grown it is larger than all the garden plants and becomes a tree, so that the birds of the air come and make nests in its branches." He told them another parable. "The kingdom of heaven is like leaven that a woman took and hid in three measures of flour, till it was all leavened."

After Jesus tells those parables, he explained about the wheat and the weeds:

> The harvest is the end of the age, and the reapers are angels. Just as the weeds are gathered and burned with fire, so will it be at the

end of the age. The Son of Man will send his angels, and they will gather out of His kingdom all causes of sin and all law-breakers, and throw them into the fiery furnace. In that place there will be weeping and gnashing of teeth. Then the righteous will shine like the sun in the kingdom of their Father. He who has ears, let him hear. (*Matthew 13:39–43*)

In a way, these stories aren't conclusive—it's unclear how big that harvest will be. It's only when we combine it with the other stories—where the leaven fills the whole loaf, and the mustard seed becomes a gigantic bush—that we have some assurance of the size of the harvest. Fortunately, so we're clear about what must take place before our Lord returns, His friend John saw a mighty vision described in the book of Revelation:

After this I looked, and behold, a great multitude that no one could number, from every nation, from all tribes and peoples and languages, standing before the throne and before the Lamb, clothed in white robes, with palm branches in their hands, and crying out with a loud voice, "Salvation belongs to our God who sits on the throne, and to the Lamb!" (*Revelation 7:9–10*)

So we know there will be people from every ethnic group, every language, around the throne of God. Since there's some 40% of the world, some seven thousand people groups, with no church in their culture right now, we know there's a ways to go!

But we also know there's an exciting development of the first chosen ethnic group returning to God, as the Messianic movement grows among the Jewish people group. And that brings us to the third Bible basis for a great harvest—greater than anything we've seen:

So I ask, did they [the Jewish people] stumble in order that they might fall? By no means! Rather, through their trespass salvation has come to the Gentiles, so as to make Israel jealous. Now if their trespass means riches for the world, and if their failure means riches for the Gentiles, how much more will their full inclusion mean! Now I am speaking to you Gentiles. Inasmuch then as I am an apostle to the Gentiles, I magnify my ministry in order somehow to make my fellow Jews jealous, and thus save some of them. For if their rejection means the reconciliation of the world, what will their acceptance mean but life from the dead? If the dough offered as firstfruits is holy, so is the whole lump, and if the root is holy, so are the branches. (*Romans 11:11–16*)

Something greater than we have known, something fuller than we have known, is coming to planet Earth when God's chosen people accept His Messiah—and it's happening. There's a building crescendo of worship from both Jews and Gentiles that will see people from every tribe worshiping, and see the whole loaf of the world filled with the yeast of the kingship of God! *That's* the biblical basis for our confidence that there's a great harvest coming!

I've heard people use the figure "a billion-soul harvest." Yet, even if all of those harvested were in the political country of India, the harvest would miss a quarter billion souls! On the other hand, is it possible that in our expectancy for the spectacular, we'll miss the yeast of the kingdom—those obscure particles that can easily be overlooked and that, once mixed with the dough, disappear from sight?

Ponder and Apply

The Lord is not slow to fulfill his promise as some count slowness, but is patient toward you, not wishing that any should perish, but that all should reach repentance. (*2 Peter 3:9*)

Are we so used to a view that focuses on remnants and how difficult it is to find the path to salvation that we can't think of a different view—a view that says God's work can be bigger than we can imagine? After telling us His

ways are different than, and higher than ours, the Lord speaks of a harvest
that will come from His very words:

> For My thoughts are not your thoughts,
> neither are your ways My ways, declares the Lord.
> For as the heavens are higher than the earth,
> so are My ways higher than your ways
> and My thoughts than your thoughts.
> For as the rain and the snow come down from heaven
> and do not return there but water the earth,
> making it bring forth and sprout,
> giving seed to the sower and bread to the eater,
> so shall My word be that goes out from my mouth;
> it shall not return to Me empty,
> but it shall accomplish that which I purpose,
> and shall succeed in the thing for which I sent it. (*Isaiah 55:8–11*)

CHAPTER 23

The Choice of Zeal: Burning Out Rather Than Rusting

He must increase, but I must decrease. He who comes from above is above all. He who is of the earth belongs to the earth and speaks in an earthly way. He who comes from heaven is above all. He bears witness to what He has seen and heard, yet no one receives His testimony. Whoever receives His testimony sets his seal to this, that God is true. For He whom God has sent utters the words of God, for He gives the Spirit without measure. (*John 3:30–34*)

No doubt if Uncle Murry was fully conversant now, he would emphasize that he was and is an earthenware vessel who responded to God's work in His life in an uncertain and limited way. We recall Mhono's letter about God choosing "weak vessels to shame the strong people." Uncle Murry may have had some mixture in motives in his zeal for mission; each of us is subject to the flesh. But nonetheless, our Lord worked in and through him. His relentless pursuit of God is actually unnerving to hear about. It's no surprise that his favorite verse would be: "Blessed is that servant whom his master will find so doing [working] when he comes" (*Luke 12:43*). And that his favorite hymn is "Will There Be Any Stars in My Crown?"

> I am thinking today of that beautiful land
>
> I shall reach when the sun goeth down
>
> When through wonderful grace by my Saviour I stand
>
> Will there be any stars in my crown?
>
> Will there be any stars, any stars in my crown?
>
> When at evening the sun goeth down
>
> When I wake with the blest in the mansions of rest
>
> Will there be any stars in my crown?[263]

As we hear about Uncle Murry's zeal, it's also fascinating to remember what the missionary C. E. Hunter's widow recounted about her husband, who we recall played a catalyzing role in the first wave of revival:

> He did work day and night—as if he had only a little while to do all the things he wanted to do. Though we both knew he wasn't well, we thought it was only the repeated attacks of dysentery which we both have had. Because he was so very tired I begged him to rest and relax on our trip home: but he always said he was all right and he wanted to finish typing the manuscript for the printers.[264]

With that in mind, we can see parallels as Mhono told about her husband's approach to mission and ministry: "When we first stayed there in Siliguri no one supported us. Only sometimes a well-wisher, or as I said, my Papa." Even Mhono's father's financial support wasn't regular but was given for particular outreach campaigns. The effect of this lack of finances was that there were times they didn't have much food. But then, because they'd developed a network of believers, guests traveling from Nepal or Bhutan would just show up at the training center. In fact, Mhono said, Ajano would serve everyone else first and sometimes get only a little or nothing at all. Mhono said all of this as a lead-in to tell about her frustration:

> So whenever I have money, I'll go and buy some good food for him, say chicken or goat. . . . I'd be ready to give him—and suddenly he would say, "I'm on a fast" *(dramatic sigh)*. THAT was the most frustrating time for me. "With great difficulty, somehow I managed to make good food for you; why are you doing this?"

When Mhono would then try to persuade him to eat, his response was, "You do not know anything about spiritual matters!" She went on, "He fasted so much. He was also a bit extreme person. Very obstinate. He doesn't take other people's advice much. Yeah, he had a good faith, great faith, in the sight of God but God loves us—not only our spirit—He loves our body also and He resides in our body." She thinks his mental decline and semi-invalid condition now are a result of his extreme approach to life and fasting. "Whether it is correct in the sight of God or not, that I still do not know, but I'm thinking is that his suffering is his own creation."

> Maybe the devil took advantage also. Because without drinking water, he used to speak five hours, sometimes even six hours. The people, even if we want to stop, the people, said "Please go on! Tell us more. Tell us more!" It was the first taste in the Sikkim area, in Darjeeling area, first taste of the word of God. Because he was a forerunner. So I think God sent him to meet the need of the people in that region. So that is also the will of God—what to do? God knows everything. So even without drinking water he spoke like this, so his whole body was dehydrated.

So Uncle Murry's devotion to God, in the form of dry fasting, led to dehydration of the brain and his physical condition now? One of his sons-in-law who studied under him at the training center in Siliguri gives a different perspective—and recounted his inspiring example of devotion:

> Every night there would be prayer for one or two hours say 8–10 or 7–9. And you know, once he [Uncle Murry] starts praying he will forget everything else. We used to sing, "So forget about yourself, (*starts singing*) so forget about yourself, concentrate on Him and worship Him. Worship Him, Christ the Lord." That forgetting about himself, that was exactly what he did. His prayer was always concentrated on this word "revival." Just "revival." Awakening. The latter rain. And he would pray nonstop for it, the movement of God. And we—young people would sometimes fall asleep. Yeah—he could sit on his knees you know—and pray for two hours nonstop—it's amazing! Then we would go to sleep and sometimes in the middle of the night, like 12, or 1, 2 o'clock, if we had to go to the bathroom we had to go outside because there was a toilet outside. And there's still light in his room, and you can still hear him, singing some melodies, or hear him in prayer, or he would be searching the scriptures—but he would be the first one to rise in the morning also! So it's not like he had a lack of sleep or—I think he ate and drank revival. That's the thing that keeps him going.

How did Uncle Murry respond to the students or staff who "couldn't keep up" with his intense prayer schedule?

> We would get scoldings sometimes, but with love. He couldn't get it—why can't we pray for revival like he can? Because it was such a clear thing for him: That's what you pray for—this is the main important thing. But other times, "Oh-oh, I think I went

too long—go to bed!" He would have that kind of response also. And then of course he's very disciplined. So he would discipline himself AND the staff sometimes. We'd come out for breakfast in the morning and find a notice on the kitchen door, "Dry fasting today" something like that (*laughing*). The Lord had showed him it was time to fast and pray. Sometimes that was a little tough on the younger generation! So there was sometimes a little bit of a generation gap, I think—or an experience gap. Spiritually. But—we survived (*laughs*)!

Asked if he thought Uncle Murry's dry fasting led to his physical and mental decline, he said:

I'm not sure if the Lord inspires you to fast, I don't think it will affect your health. But there might be times when putting it on yourself—then there must be some price maybe attached to that. So I don't know—I'm not saying that he did everything led by the Spirit, I mean he's a human being. So I can imagine that it affected his health. Because certain things might be lacking.[265]

Another close observer of Uncle Murry's life is Prashant Thapa, now lead pastor of River of Living Waters Fellowship, Darjeeling. He had been a Hindu acolyte as a young teen, before starting to follow Jesus. At age 42, he shared his memories of Uncle Murry, starting when he met him as a 17-year-old:

When Uncle Murry came here as a missionary, by the grace of God I personally could meet him. From that day onward, Uncle Murry started mentoring me. He took me to the high places—where he used to spend hours praying. And I had to follow—had to watch him closely since I had never seen such kind of a person before. Always singing, always praying in tongues, always lifting up holy hands, declaring his Kingdom.

Uncle Murry rented a single room near Prashant's family's small wooden home. He'd spend a good amount of time with them, praying, sharing the word, eating together. Prashant remembered "praying and singing in tongues A LOT," as well as declaring the Lord's kingship over the Hindu temples and high places. He also spoke of Uncle Murry's fasting:

> He used to fast for 40 days, sometimes one week, sometime 21 days. Then he used to pray for revival. Revival had hold of his heart. He used to always talk about revival and sing revival songs. "I want revival in my soul." I still remember, he used to teach us a lot of revival songs. And I have taught these songs to my children also. He was such a crazy man, I had never seen that kind of man before—he has had a great impact in my life.

Prashant went on to describe the fruit of his fasting:

> The most important thing was the demons used to flee. There were incredible miracles that took place. We used to visit different homes with Uncle Murry. And every fellowship, the demons used to be cast out—healings used to take place—after Uncle Murry came, that was the time so many conversions take place. When he used to pray for revival, that was the time. Even now we don't see as many conversions. But during that specific period, when Uncle used to visit here, so many souls got saved. So many souls got saved and impacted.

Prashant went on to describe how he emulated Uncle Murry because he saw walking with God was the most important thing in life:

> I gave up all entertainment. And I was solely focused and I used to do whatever Uncle Murry used to do. I myself started fasting, all by myself. I started in a very small way like three days without water. Staying inside the room for three days without even

drinking water, spending time with the Lord. So I was very, very serious.

If "three days without water" is "starting in a small way," we get a vivid picture of the example he'd seen. As part of mentoring Prashant, Uncle Murry took him to Nagaland in 1997 to preach there. Uncle Murry had hoped Prashant could do some of the driving, but he hadn't learned how yet!

He took me to different Baptist churches. As a young man, I could speak on revival. So yeah, the mantle was on me also. When I used to preach revival, people used to confess their sins. They used to come forward, and the testimonies used to come—they have quit smoking, they have given up adulterous life, young people they used to cry, they used to return back to the Lord. So yeah, great things happened. I used to preach a lot about revival, and automatically, people used to repent.

Prashant had grown up without a father and hadn't experienced a father's love until he encountered Uncle Murry: "When he came into my life he came not just as a spiritual father, but he came as an earthly father also. We had a very strong relationship." Asked if he'd seen Uncle Murry's health decline:

One thing I noticed in his life is that he would sing a lot, all the time. Twenty-four hours he used to sing, if he was not sleeping. While driving, while walking, even at house. Maybe because of that, God has added to his years. If other people were in his position, they would have died. So I believe that even now God has kept him, even if his health is not good, God has just kept him alive, because his singing is very powerful. And the singing that he does is creating an atmosphere. It will drive out demons—so God will keep him on this earth as long as He wants so that he can fulfill the assignment, the task, that he has received.[266]

With that singing in mind, Uncle Murry's own words from his Latter Rain Revival Ministry newsletter dated January 1993 are an appropriate closing:

The six months ministry in Sikkim assigned to me by the Lord is now over. But my love for Sikkim has never been abandoned, and my prayer ministry will ever be afresh. My earthly body is becoming weaker and older, but my spirit in the Lord is stronger, and I'm praying to go again and walk over again in the spirit of Elijah, who walked with God and walked over to heaven. Enoch who walked with God and walked over to heaven. Praise the Lord, Peter while walking in spirit could go on walking on water, but when he turned to flesh, he sank. Walking with the spirit of God I can go anywhere—

"But until then my heart will go on singing,
Until then with joy I'll carry on,
Until that day, my eyes behold that city,
Until that day, God calls me home." Amen.[267]

Ponder and Apply

His disciples remembered that it was written, "Zeal for your house will consume me." *(John 2:17)*

I have become a stranger to my brothers,
an alien to my mother's sons.
Zeal for your house has consumed me;
the insults aimed at you have landed on me.
I wept bitterly while I fasted
and exposed myself to insults.
I have made sackcloth my clothing
and become a byword among the people.

Those who sit by the town gate gossip about me;
I am the theme of drunken songs.
At an acceptable time
I lift my prayer to you, LORD.
In your great and enduring love
answer me, God, with sure deliverance. (*Psalm 69:8-13, REB*)

Obviously Uncle Murry's life of singing—or worship—is an example of what *to do*. So, at least in some way, is his habit of fasting. Living a fasting lifestyle is associated with seeing more of God, in relationship and direction and power. We can ponder the questions: Did Uncle Murry go too far? Did C. E. Hunter go too far? But where does our pondering lead us?

Let's also look at what *not to do*. What saps (or zaps!) our zeal? What opens the door wider to obvious temptation? Here are three Bs to watch for that tell us there's an issue with our zeal:

Boredom—When we aren't entranced by the wonder and marvels of God, our minds can look for ungodly stimulation. We're designed to be entranced and excited during times of our life—that's why walking and hearing from our Lord is an adventure! When it's not, there's a problem!

Barrenness—Our Lord created us for fruitfulness, whether that's growth in character in our own life or being part of changing the people and situations around us. When we think we're barren, we can begin looking for fulfillment in the wrong places. Instead, let's find God's perspective and be grateful for the opportunities we've had to reflect our Lord's glory, of being good to people around us.

Busyness (or distraction)—It's not being "busy" in particular that's the problem, but when the "busyness" becomes a distraction:

A woman named Martha welcomed him into her house. And she had a sister called Mary, who sat at the Lord's feet and listened to his teaching. But Martha was distracted with much serving. And she went up to him and said, "Lord, do you not care that my sister has left me to serve alone? Tell her then to help me." But the Lord answered her, "Martha, Martha, you are anxious and troubled about many things, but one thing is necessary. Mary has chosen the good portion, which will not be taken away from her." (*Luke 10:38b–42*)

CHAPTER 24

Sustaining Revival

But you, my son, have observed closely my teaching and manner of life, my resolution, my faithfulness, patience and spirit
of love and my fortitude under persecution and suffering. . . .
But for your part, stand by the truths you have learned and are
assured of. . . . And now there awaits me the garland of righteousness which the Lord, the righteous Judge, will award to
me on the great day, and not to me alone but all who have set
their hearts on His coming appearance. (*2 Timothy 3:10–11,
14; 4:8, REB*)

Our title is *Sustaining Revival*, which implies a question: How does one
sustain revival?

Or, depending upon how we intone the words, the question might be:
How does revival sustain us?

It's a continuing drama and process—which we can see through many
years of God's Spirit working in our Nagaland family. Yes, they are a family
who may be different from ours in culture, but not so much that we can't

identify with the very human struggles and weaknesses they exhibited and overcame.

Or, we could ask the two questions in terms of Uncle Murry: How much was Uncle Murry being carried by the effects of the Spirit's power in his life—and how much was Uncle Murry hungering after more of God?

Or to apply it to ourselves: How much of the continuing work of the Spirit is a person's responsibility? Does human action matter in terms of prolonging or even inviting works of the Holy Spirit?

At one extreme, we could see our actions as determinative and potentially, in theory, allowing for the possibility of living in continuous revival. At the other extreme, we could become passive and conclude that people play no role in seeing our Lord move.

> *Interviewer:* The reason I'm focusing on this question of what happened before the revival is that many people think that there's a prayer movement before revival.
>
> *Ajano:* Were there any people who were praying here?
>
> *Mhono:* That's why I am thinking it is a special grace of God, because at that time nobody knew about revival. And nobody—yeah, of course, praying, prayer must be there because the missionaries taught us how to pray, must have taught us how to pray. But—we— those people, elderly people, they did not know the deeper things of God. The violent faith. They never knew the violent faith. So, must be some people praying—that we do not know.

When Mhono speaks of "violent faith," she's referring to Jesus's words in Matthew 11:12: "From the days of John the Baptist until now the kingdom of heaven has suffered violence, and the violent take it by force." But what is knowing "the deeper things" she speaks of?

One "deeper" pattern that shows up in His Word is seeing that just as seasons are part of natural creation, seasons are part of the spiritual calendar as well. As we ponder the lives of this family in Nagaland who responded in the way they did to Holy Spirit's work, as did many others, we can conclude they lived well in the season they were offered. It's fascinating that in our four days with Mhono, she never shared any particular revival experience of her own, other than when she received an individual word of encouragement when she was going through a personal hell-on-earth in the mid-1970s. She lived out her devotion to our Lord, not based on anything more spectacular, evidently, than any other believer has enjoyed.

Another "deeper" aspect is the incredible and crucial place of humility in our declarations about God's ways. I've read absolute, categorical statements about the necessity of united prayer before He moves in a demonstrable way in revival—and yet, God is God. Evidently, if He wants to move among Nagas who haven't asked and are characterized by spiritual lukewarmness, He can! We are always and continually students of His ways—and always have something to learn.

With that heart in mind, here's one more example of our Lord's work in this family: Mhono and Yaniethung Murry were both in West Bengal at one point, and received a call from Mhono's father: "You have to come—the Lord has said I have forty days and then He's coming to take me." At this point, Merithung was weak and unable to run the school, but not ill. Of course they did return to Nagaland, and he entered eternity exactly forty days after he'd been told he would.[268] Something equally unusual happened in another revivalist's family, when Lano Longchar's mother died in 1979 as the third wave of the Spirit was cresting:

> An angel of the Lord told Longchar's mother that many people will come to their place the next day and to keep the surroundings clean and keep everything ready. . . . She did everything as she was told. . . . Lano's eldest brother, who was a pastor, along with his two sisters were with their mother. . . .They spent the whole night sharing the joy of the Lord and how God had been faithful to them. Then at exactly three o'clock in the morning, without any sign of

sickness or pain, his mother said, "I am now ready to go" and she then breathed her last.[269]

She had gotten the house clean—for her own funeral, which in accord with local custom, took place the next day. To top off the event, the next day one hundred fellow villagers were touched by the Holy Spirit and converted.[270]

Another aspect of that humility is reality about our own hearts. When we say, "We need revival," is it possible that the problem is the plural pronoun? Is it really "we," or am I really thinking, "*They* need revival"? Maybe a key step for us is to be able to say, "*I* need revival," and focus on that. That focus might allow each of us individually to embrace the tension—a tension we can describe as: let's live revived, and continue to seek more!

A preeminent preacher of the nineteenth century mentioned earlier because his books were in such demand during the 1857–58 awakening in New York City, Charles Spurgeon, said something which expands on this tension:

> Ought we not to look upon our own history as being at least as full of God . . . as the lives of any of the saints who have gone before? We do our Lord an injustice when we suppose that He wrought all His mighty acts, and showed Himself strong for those in the early time, but doth not perform wonders or lay bare His arm for the saints who are now upon the earth.[271]

Perhaps as we read Spurgeon's words, there's a sense that what he's saying applies to other people but not to us. We haven't enjoyed the season of grace the Naga believers enjoyed—or have we? Or more importantly, can we still? Of course we can, because as Spurgeon also said:

> When people hear about what God used to do one of the things they say is, "Oh that was a very long while ago." I thought it was

God that did it? Has God changed? Is He not an immutable God—
the same yesterday, today and forever? Does not that furnish an
argument to prove that what God has done at one time He can do
at another. Nay, I think that I may push it a little further, and say
that what He has done once, is a prophecy of what He intends to
do again.[272]

May His work among the Naga tribes be repeated throughout our
world! Come, Lord Jesus!

Afterword

Stories of revival are among my favorite things to read. They have a way of awakening us to faith, inciting us to spiritual hunger, and calling us out of compromise and mediocrity. Hearing the stories of past moves of God can spark moves of God in our own lives today. No doubt this was one of the hopes my friend carried when he wrote this special book.

On more than a few occasions my jaw dropped while reading this manuscript. I recall the record of the many birds entering the homes of villagers in different regions to announce *"Jesus is coming soon!"* in the people's respective dialects! The hundred thousand–plus gathered to hear the gospel and experience the miracles. Or the supernatural retribution against those who lifted their hand against God's people.

These accounts blew my mind.

These are not normal stories of the harvest. They are unusual accounts of God expressing His glory in both his kindness and His severity (Romans 11:22). While these occurrences may seem outrageous or even conflict with our contemporary image of *revival*, they are nevertheless clear manifestations of the glory of God—revival!

The stories of Nagaland have stirred in me a fresh longing for the inbreaking of God's glory today. We desperately need the fullness of His glory—both His hand of salvation as well as His hand of discipline. If the

Father's salvation is what transfers us to the kingdom of the Son, it's the Father's discipline that keeps us there.

Oh that the glory of God would rise upon us again!

There seems to be a growing number of leaders speaking of imminent harvest in our day. With the backdrop of international shakings (Hebrews 12:26) via a global pandemic, racial unrest, sexual confusion, and political polarization, many believe our current darkness is primed for an invasion of God's glory.

> Behold, darkness shall cover the earth and thick darkness the peoples; but the LORD will arise upon you, and his glory will be seen upon you. (*Isaiah 60:2*)

The question is: *Is the church prepared?*

I am reminded of a fresh story from my friend Pastor Brandon Naramore (Rock of Roseville, California). He tells about a recent conversion of a young adult in his fellowship. While on a drug high this young man was taken into a heavenly vision where he met Jesus, who called him to be a farmer in His harvest. The young man came out of the vision completely sober, born again, and immediately activated in preaching the gospel with miracles and signs following him!

Pastor Brandon recalls a conversation he had with God about this young man.

"Lord, someone needs to mentor this kid. Someone needs to disciple him."

"You do it," the Lord replies.

"I don't have time! I'm mentoring leaders and running this church."

The Lord immediately responded with a question, *"Did Dan Mohler have time for Todd White?"* (Two evangelists who move in the supernatural.)

You can bet what happened next. Pastor Brandon entered into a mentorship relationship with this young man. He's now deeply invested in his spiritual growth and discipling him in the way of Jesus.

Pastor Brandon is a model for all of us.

If the glory of God is to rise upon the church today, we must believe it will be accompanied by thousands of these kinds of salvation stories. We will see sinners swept out of lifestyles of addiction, sin, and confusion. They will come from every sphere of society and yet they will all come with one common, glaring need: discipleship.

Each of them will need to be taught the way of Jesus. They will have needs of freedom, healing, and deliverance. They will need space to serve, to discover the grace of God on their lives, and to take steps into their unique purpose. For all of this, each of them will need a community that embodies and demonstrates the kingdom, and leaders who are willing to make rich deposits into their lives with God.

Are we ready to make this kind of discipleship investment in the lives of new Jesus followers?

A true vision for the harvest forces us to also think in terms of church reformation. For if we accept that the glory of God is to rise upon us resulting in many salvations (revival), we must orient ourselves (reformation) for the demands that the harvest will place on us. Jesus's words carry this same vision:

> The harvest is plentiful but the laborers are few. Therefore, pray earnestly to the Lord of the harvest to send out laborers into his harvest. (*Luke 10:2*)

The God-story from Nagaland speaks to us today. It challenges our preconceptions about revival and sobers us with a view of the cost that comes with it. In some ways this book plays the same role as that of the birds in Nagaland. It comes to us as a gripping supernatural sign and declares, *"Jesus is coming soon!"*

May we respond to this message with prophetic unction and prepare for the greatest move of God the world has ever seen.

Adam Narciso
Jesus Movement Now
Nashville, Tennessee, USA

PART 3

Appendices

We've looked at the waves and flow of revival in one area, focusing on one group of tribes, through the life experience of one family. We've looked deeper at several themes that emerged and considered how they speak to how we live today.

For those who want to explore this supernatural work of our Lord more fully, let's look further at three topics.

Mission: The Fruit Which Prolongs Revival

> And when these lepers came to the edge of the camp, they went into a tent and ate and drank, and they carried off silver and gold and clothing and went and hid them. . . . Then they said to one another, "We are not doing right. This day is a day of good news. If we are silent and wait until the morning light, punishment will overtake us. Now therefore come; let us go and tell the king's household." (*2 Kings 7:8–9*)

Often when our Lord touches people supernaturally, mission is the result. One says "often" because it's not uniform or absolute, but when people are touched they become more like Jesus—and He's on a mission. Jesus came for a twofold mission: to seek and save the lost (Luke 19:10) and to destroy the works of the evil one (1 John 3:8b). We can unify these two missions into one aim: making disciples—followers who know Him and are growing more like Him.

So when our Lord moves in a way which can be described as revival, mission often emerges. In fact, it's precisely in mission efforts that we see the work of the Holy Spirit continue with the power which birthed them. While we've examined how division comes, particularly as new wineskins are needed to live out the new experience of God, Holy Spirit's work can also bring unprecedented unity—in mission. A history of the Baptist churches in Nagaland and the surrounding states of northeast India, while addressing their mission and church history up to the 1950s, still could be applied to the immediate effects of God's move—whether in the '50s, '60s or the '70s—of inspiring outreach and mission to other tribes. One writer both remembers and laments in the same passage:

> Another fact about the early history of our church [the Baptist churches in northeast India] cannot fail to impress any student of it. This was the sense of unity in a common cause. These were men and women for whom the phrase "One in Christ" really meant something. Assamese left their safe homes to risk their lives— and certainly their comforts—preaching among the suspicious, often hostile hillsmen. Aos and Angamis were not primarily concerned about the members of their own tribes when they travelled among the villages of neighboring tribes that were their traditional enemies. Kuki and Naga worked side by side in evangelizing the hill people of Manipur. They were conscious of belonging to a new community infinitely more important than their natural communities, a community with a single work to do. Christianity was, in those days, the strongest force for unity that existed in the region. Perhaps it was their common suffering, perhaps it was because they were living closer to the essence of the gospel, that through this community, poor in material resources and in qualified leadership as the world—and we ourselves—tend to judge such matters today, God was able to work miracles. Apart from this unity it would have been difficult if not impossible for Him to accomplish what He did.[273] The greatest tragedy in our history has

not been the suffering, the frequent backsliding, the lost opportunities—the greatest tragedy has been the gradual erosion of this early sense of unity.[274]

The organizing of the Nagaland Christian Revival Church in the '60s could be seen as an example of the loss of unity (particularly from a Baptist perspective, since they were leaving Baptist churches), or we could see it as simply a "new wineskin," a normal fruit of a move of the Spirit. Certainly mission was a big part of the NCRC history in the beginning among different tribes within Nagaland, but even early in their history we can see mission beyond the state's borders:

> In 1963 at Sastami, a police personnel Mr. Krishna Nepali[275] was posted at V. K. town. He attended the church one evening and the Holy Spirit fell upon him and [he] was wonderfully saved. While he was taking water baptism, the water in which he was immersing appeared like blood and a rainbow encircled him. All the believers who were standing at the bank were the witnesses. A woman prophesied that he is chosen to serve the Lord with persecution. True to the revelation his wife left him because of his faith. He resigned from the government service and went back to his native place Nepal to preach the gospel.[276]

This particular form of mission involved returning to one's native place and sharing what God has done in your life. In this case, someone originally from Nepal went back there to share—because God had touched him in Nagaland.

But another form of mission is to go away from one's native place, and take the news to people who aren't like you. In other words, someone from one culture senses God directing them to go and reach another cultural group. Initially, among the Nagas, this impulse carried the news from members of one tribe to those of another, but still geographically quite close. Eventually, the mission impulse carried Naga believers beyond their immediate territory. Uncle Murry was one of many Nagas called out of Nagaland by our Lord.

Inevitably, there's spiritual opposition to the expansion of our Lord's authority in an area or people group. We've recounted how Uncle Murry encountered opposition during his land purchase, but that wasn't the only time. And just as the Holy Spirit had launched him and guided him in the past years of revival, our Lord continued to protect and confirm his efforts. His son David remembered during those early days in Siliguri:

> While we were setting up, he faced a lot of trouble and problems. There were some gangsters; one man came and threatened him— he [Uncle Murry] would put his hands on them and pray for them.
>
> Mr. Sharma and three bodyguards came with some problem. So in the middle of the conversation Sharma goes on the floor. He's knocked out by the spirit of God, and his bodyguards were really nervous and didn't know what to do. His bodyguards helped him up and left, and never bothered him. The area people feared him, "There's something different about Uncle Murry." Neighbors would bother him, and he would rebuke the devil.[277]

Uncle Murry's approach to mission reflected how his spiritual life had been formed through both revival and revival messages:

Interviewer: So now a separate spiritual question, how did he combine . . . his campaigns in Sikkim and Darjeeling and so on were often denouncing sin and he would spend quite a bit of time attacking sin, and yet he was such a man of unconditional love that he would forgive people who ripped him off for a thousand rupees, or a hundred thousand rupees?

Uncle Murry's son-in-law: See, he knew that denouncing sin was a preparatory work that needed to be done for God's presence to be strong in the meeting and . . . so that God could work unhindered. So that would have been the reason that he would do that first.

Interviewer: A John the Baptist, "Prepare ye thè way?"

Uncle Murry's son-in-law: Yes. It's the both sides. You do that and then it prepares hearts. Prepares the fallow ground. It opens people up. It makes people realize, they do need salvation, they do need forgiveness, they need—you know, there is that part, but he would have the other side of the gospel of course, just as much, or even more, that there is salvation, there is forgiveness, there is Holy Spirit baptism, there is healing. There is deliverance, which would be very much evidenced in his campaigns. So—so you end with that.

He would be hurt, it would really hurt him—I remember one occasion when he came back from a campaign or actually a crusade somewhere in the hills and he had paid for everything—I didn't go to the campaign myself, I wasn't there, but I was there when he prepared it with the pastors and I was there when the pastors were saying that several thousand people will attend and we'll provide lunch for them and we need a big stage, we need ambulances to be able to come and go and everything was prepared. And there was a huge budget for that. Maybe several lakhs [hundred thousands] of rupees. So he had raised this money and he went to Nagaland and raised some money, maybe he sold a piece of land, whatever he did for that, invest the whole money, gave them and they started preparing and then sometimes there was a meeting with only three or four hundred people present instead of three or four thousand—you know. So you would think you would have money left over from lunch, right? According to the calculations. But no money would ever return to him. I mean ever in the times that I have seen it, which was only after 2003, 2004. No money would return and one time he came back with taxi and not even the taxi was paid for! They arranged the taxi for him to come back to Siliguri and the driver said, after dropping him here at the gate, eight hours there, "Uhh Uncle,"—he left the taxi, said "Thank you so much," he left and then you know the driver said, "Hey, Uncle, you need to— pay!" "Oh, it was not arranged, I thought it was. . . . " "No, they said you would pay!" So he still had to pay the whatever, the 3,000 something for the taxi. Those kind of things, I mean what is 3,000 compared to 3 lakhs [300,000]? But—it should have been included. So it's sometimes those little things that become very painful. But he would forgive them you know, but he might not do a crusade again with them. You know in that way.

But it was also, for me, personally, it was something—he would tell me—in the beginning he would tell me, "You will also do like this. You will also go for crusades. You will also pray for the sick." Things like that. But I myself did not find this same call, as a crusade or convention speaker.

But I was much more inclined to training others and maybe it's my thrifty thinking, that instead of three lakhs [hundred thousand rupees] for a crusade, we can support a church planter for three years. With the same amount of money on a constant weekly basis, people can hear the gospel instead of three days. So in that way it did make sense to me that we should train people. It made sense to him also. Because one of the reasons he wanted to start training was that people had come back to him, several years after the crusade, they said, "Uncle, we were blessed, we were healed, we were born again during the crusade and we went to the local churches as you have told us to do but we still don't know how to pray!" Several years later we have not been taught. We have not been taught. This is when the Lord really began to give him the responsibility of saying, "Hey you're responsible also for the ones you have led to me, you also are responsible to nurture them. In me. In Christ." Their spiritual well-being, you know.

Initially we would be partnering with the local churches that are present maybe and trying to increase their harvest. Let them share in the harvest, which is the right thing to do I think but at the same time some of those churches are not teaching the Word, you know, and they're not discipling people, and sometimes they didn't even look after the ones that were brought to the Lord. So what are you doing then, are you just leaving it or are you taking up that responsibility? And he decided that we should take up the responsibility and start looking for training partners, and that's how we have started, you know having short-term and longer-term courses, to raise up more younger people. And another reason was that he was becoming older so who is going to look after them in all those different places? So he felt we should raise up younger people with the same revival heart and vision who would nurture those who have come into the kingdom. So this is the reason why we are having training programs over here.[278]

Interviewer: During this period [roughly 2005–2015], did he go back and forth?

Uncle Murry's son-in-law: Yes.

Interviewer: And he was restless—if he was here, he wanted to be there . . . ?

Uncle Murry's son-in-law: Yeah, he didn't really want to be there, but he couldn't really be here—something like that physically. He always wants to be here, but sometimes he cannot. And so yeah, he would go back and forth. Whenever, he would come back we would try to organize some crusades or something for him, during those years. He did still a few, but the last five years, ten years, we have not been able to hold major crusades. He did a few meetings with Parbesh, you know, the earlier trained students; they are more fresh in his memory than the latest ones, because he was more involved with them. And he loved to sing, one of the great gifts that he has is that he loves to sing. Even now also, he will sing.[279]

Indeed, if one fruit which sustained revival fire in Uncle Murry was mission, singing in worship appears to be another. One evening our interviewing team had the privilege of seeing the despair and discouragement in Uncle Murry's heart as he was looking at his own life! And what were the two hallmarks we saw and heard? Mission and music!

Ajano (translating for her dad): "I have become like that fig tree without fruit—I came here and I do NOTHING!" Of course it's very difficult when every day he wants to come to Siliguri—every day. Not any day misses without him thinking of coming—because of health reasons, my dad also could not do so much. Mom used to come, and stay there for some time and then come back because Dad could not stay there, could not work also—only pray. Now he's saying that because he's here he could not do anything: "While I'm here I have not done anything. So I'm like the fig tree; Jesus went and saw the fig tree, and he cursed the fig tree when he didn't see any fruit there. So I think God will feel bad with me. Jesus will feel bad with me." Because of that he suffers like this.

Why he said like that is that he cannot live without God, without doing anything for Him: "it is very good [to go] where gospel is not preached." He's now not thinking only of India, Nepal, from before he used to say "It will be very good if you can go and reach China, Russia, more, North Korea. South Korea there is some Christians, but in North Korea"—like that he's saying.

A training center graduate: "Uncle, I'm going to China."

Ajano (translating again): "The only [thing] that makes me sad is that I did not complete my work. It feels like it's not complete...."

Because of his health, he has so much desire but because of his health he could not complete it. *(pause)* He's very happy that you encourage him.

The graduate proceeds to tell her story to Uncle Murry. She comes from a different tribe, another part of Nagaland. Since she doesn't speak the Lotha language, she tells in English how she had just heard briefly about the training center, didn't even know its name but knew she wanted to go Siliguri for the training—five hundred miles from her home. She says the training changed her life as she learned about Holy Spirit and freedom of worship. After this encouragement, Ajano continued:

Ajano (translating for her dad): "God's will and His love, he's telling you, take the love and go, and then God will work, the love of God."

Graduate: Thank you Uncle, I will.

Ajano (translating for her dad): "If you go there, God will work mightily—you will love your enemies, like yourself. That's what the Word of God says. If you love, God will work mightily. Just like the song says, 'Love is the flag in the castle in my heart.'"

Both of them singing in English: Let the whole world know, let the whole world know, the flag flies high in the sky that the King is (in residence there).

Ajano (translating for her dad): "That will be the kingdom of God, where the love of God is, that will be the kingdom of God. The king is resident there with the love of God. The best is to serve God, and if you have the love of God in your heart, you'll be like a bird flying, like a bird flying everywhere, and that's the best, you know to serve God! He wanted to fly like a bird, everywhere. . . ." He's saying, if you *(the graduate)* are going to China it will be like going on his behalf. . . .

"The east and north part of the world not reached for the gospel yet. There will be some Christians, but few. . . . He anointed my head with oil, my cup runneth over, just like that, running over, it's like filling up again, and God will work mightily. . . ." He's not sad, he says *(explaining his tears)* but the love of God is filling him—that's why—thinking about the love of God he's feeling like this . . . always concerned about Russia and China, always praying—like that.[280]

APPENDIX 2

Another Wave?

Will you not revive us again,

That your people may rejoice in you? (*Psalm 85:6*)

As we consider the obvious social problems in Nagaland, and the history of incredible Holy Spirit activity, it's reasonable to ask: Will our Lord send another wave?

While certainly the form, such as week-long special meetings, and the language of "revival" is present throughout the church in Nagaland, the supernatural doesn't seem much in evidence.

With that atmosphere in mind, Thungbemo Murry, one of Uncle Murry's sons, pointed the interviewers to a possible harbinger of change—a ministry asking the church in Nagaland to fulfill their covenant with God. The reader can recall that chapter 10, "High Tide of the Spirit," closed with the ringing declaration of T. Alemmeren Ao, leader of the Nagaland Baptist Church Council at the time, representing the overwhelming number of believers in the state. He said in 1977 that they would enlist ten thousand volunteers for Christ, for the cause of world evangelization. This was a bold commitment. To get some perspective on exactly how bold, consider this statistic on a couple of nations known for sending cross-cultural workers: the U.S. and South Korea. South Korea, in 2010, sent out 1,014 missionaries per million church members; the United States sent 614 per million.[281] Since Nagaland has about two-thirds of a million church members, to achieve this goal, they would be sending out fifteen thousand missionaries per million church members—fifteen times South Korea's rate!

A little more than thirty years later T. Alemmeren Ao was interviewed about the declaration by Wabang Longchari and his Sinai Ministry team:

How did the vision to send out 10,000 volunteers for World Missions come about?

Rev. Alemmeren: In the '60s and '70s, more than 5,000 Nagas had already sacrificed their lives for the Naga cause,[282] so I was convicted by God "why not double the number and send 10,000 volunteers for the Lord's Ministry for World Missions"?

In the original documents it is recorded to enlist 10,000 Volunteers for the World Missions. What do you mean by "10,000 Volunteers"?

Rev. Alemmeren: In the resolution "Volunteers" means those people who will voluntarily come forward to be a missionary. Who are willing to surrender their life to God for the rest of their life. There is a cost and price to be paid even up to the extent of losing blood, so you need to voluntarily come to be enlisted among the 10,000 to be sent, and not because your church/parents want you to go.[283]

After a couple of questions clarifying that the number was only to include workers going from Nagaland to the unreached in other cultures, several key questions were asked:

Do you think the promise has been fulfilled?

Rev. Alemmeren: No, it is not fulfilled yet.

What did you do about this promise we made to God?

Rev. Alemmeren: After the resolution was passed and the promise was made to send 10,000, eventually the different associations under NBCC (Nagaland Baptist Church Council) resolved, and signed the resolution. In the year 1993, after my tenure got over as Director in [of] Nagaland Missionary Movement (now it is Nagaland Missions Movement), since not many were responding to go on World Mission, I was convicted and decided to move to Hong Kong with my whole family without having a clue where to stay. The first couple of days, my whole family was sleeping under a bridge. We have already celebrated 25 years of ministry in Hong Kong.

What if we don't fulfill the promise we made with God to send 10,000 Missionaries for the World Missions?

Rev. Alemmeren: God will not bless Nagaland.[284]

It is striking that the official website of the Nagaland Baptist Church Council appears to contradict and even downplay the importance of the promise, by saying it wasn't a resolution:

The Naga Mission consciousness was further heightened by the "prophetic call" in the 1970s by leaders of the NBCC, to send out 10,000 Missionaries. Though it was not the NBCC resolution as such, nevertheless, this "prophetic voice" was carried out to all the corners of Nagaland and to the world which became another catalyst for the Naga Mission. [285]

On the same website, the Nagaland Baptist Church Council states their baptized membership is 663,236, with 721 ordained ministers and 1,654 churches.[286] So while we know it was a bold commitment, it becomes more approachable when we see that the commitment involves each local church sending just six missionaries. Some churches have already done above and beyond that—Jotsama Baptist Church, a church in the Angami tribe, has sent thirty-one missionaries to eight different mission fields from 1949 to 2005.[287] Uncle Murry and his family are an additional five who wouldn't be included in any particular church's list. But despite the impressive response by some, there's no question the goal hasn't been achieved. Besides Alemmeren, Wabang told how the team talked to two other key Baptist officials who agreed that the commitment hadn't been fulfilled:

> We went to Nagaland Missions Movement Director . . . which is the mission agency under NBCC in Dimapur. We went and sat with him and asked him, "Sir, have you fulfilled it?" He said, "No, we have yet to fulfill it." Originally, we just sent missionaries under NBCC, it was 1,000 something. And if you bring, independent churches or other denominations, individuals, those who have been sent by families or private ministries, if you bring all of them together—not even half. In fact, not even 4,000. I don't know whether we have reached 3,000. We still have a long way to go.[288]

Later Wabang declared, answering those who've tried to downplay the commitment:

> If it was just an emotional covenant that we Nagas had made in 1977 then I don't think God would have bothered to speak to me on the 21st of May, 2018, when I was attending a missions conference called "Burning Hearts," in Lüdenscheid in Germany, that the Nagas have an unfinished covenant with God: which is to send 10,000 missionaries into the world!
>
> My dear fellow Nagas, today our land is in such a pathetic condition, with rampant corruption, disunity, lack of good covenants, lack of upright leaders, both political and spiritual, no development and no political solutions. Is it because *(his voice cracking)* we have forgotten the covenant we made with God? The

Lord is reminding us from Psalm 105, verse 7 and 8, "He is the LORD our God, His judgments are in all the earth. He remembers His covenants forever, the word which He commanded for a thousand generations."[289]

No doubt Wabang's call for the believers in Nagaland is to look outward. To join our Lord in His mission to those who have yet to respond is key to another wave.

Is it possible that after revival we can forget that it was a means to something—to more of Jesus's kingship expressed here on earth, and not an end in itself?

What About Head-Hunting?

That is why it is called Babel, because there the Lord made a babble of the language of the whole world. It was from that place the Lord scattered people over the face of the earth. (*Genesis 11:9, REB*)

In past generations he allowed all the nations to walk in their own ways. (*Acts 14:16*)

This writer had the privilege of sitting in on a multi-ethnic Bible class in 2018 at the training center Uncle Murry founded in Siliguri.

The students were having a "talent night," demonstrating songs, dances, or other performing arts. There were four students from the Konyak tribe of Nagaland. They did a pantomime where a headhunter raided a village and killed a baby and child. Then a pastor came to the bereaved father and consoled him, evidently encouraging him that the only recourse was to forgive!

As I sat and watched this tale unfold, I realized while that exact drama may not have happened, there's no doubt the thrust of the pantomime was historically true! There had to be victims who said, "We won't retaliate, we'll forgive," as the good news of Christ penetrated the Naga tribes.

Since a state of ongoing murderous raids between tribes is so foreign to Western readers' current experience, the author is making this an appendix to our main story. Our main thrust is to focus on what might apply to us in understanding God's wholesale supernatural intervention in a society. By the time of the 1950 revivals, head-hunting was disappearing. Certainly the taking of heads had affected the spread of the kingship of God among the Nagas. As late as 1948 the American Baptist worker C. E. Hunter related this in his annual report:

> Until August I was not allowed to visit the second range of the Sangtam villages but GOVERNMENT PERMISSION WAS AT LAST GIVEN TO ENTER THE TRIBAL AREA. After the meeting of the Sangtam Association in November, I visited the new government station in that area at Tuensang—the first visit of a missionary ever made into this wild territory. Shortly before my visit the warriors of the large village near the Government station decided to go on a headhunting raid, but were dissuaded by two of our Naga Christian government officials. One upper Konyak or Bhom village lost nearly 100 heads, mainly of women and children, in a raid this year. Daos or knives are used for decapitation, but first the victims were shot with village-made guns.[290]

Hunter mentioned head-hunting briefly in a letter to Dr. J. E. Skoglund, dated May 6, 1950:

> More head-hunting is reported not far from Impur among the Phom (Upper Konyak) villages where Ao gospel teams recently toured, although there is no connection between the two![291]

Then again in another letter to Skoglund, dated June 28, 1950:

A head-hunting raid prevented a gospel team from visiting more than three of the Phom or Upper Konyak villages, where several churches have been established since last November by gospel team trips of four Ao churches near the border. This is the last great stronghold of head-hunting in the areas near Impur. I pointed out the majestic mountain on the East from which the head hunters went when you were here—standing in our front yard; it is quite striking since its top is bell-shaped.

His mention that victims, at least in this one case in this time period, were shot first, is an interesting if macabre detail. There's no mention of guns in a *National Geographic* video about two Konyak headhunters still living in recent times titled "Why These Head Hunters Converted to Christianity." After telling how he killed people and cut off their heads, Wangloi Wangshu is translated as saying "When the Christian missionaries came to my village, they asked me if I was a son of God. I replied, 'Yes, I am.' It seemed like a good idea to keep the peace rather than kill each other."

The other head-hunter shown is Hongo Konyak:

I changed my mind when I heard preaching from a pastor and when I read through the Bible. These things are what changed my mind. I don't miss the old traditions much because they weren't good traditions. At the same time I don't regret anything I've done in the past. I don't regret those things. I don't regret those things. We have kept the good things in our tradition, and let the bad things go. We, the Konyaks, have a strong culture. We have had customary law for a long time so we will not stop having our culture.[292]

The only additional explanation on the video about this incredible spiritual change comes from Wantin Kano, identified as the Lungwa pastor (or Longwa—a Konyak village which straddles the border of Myanmar and India). He said: "When the Christian missionary came to the Konyak tribe, some people said they weren't going to accept the religion. But some agreed to when they saw the way the people from the outside lived. Slowly changes came to this land. Now 90% of Konyaks have accepted Christianity."[293]

No doubt each of those three men's explanations of how change came to the Konyak tribe gives part of the picture. Yet I trust that our survey of the work of God in Nagaland shows another explanation: There was an incredible supernatural intervention that propelled people from different tribes to travel and cross language and cultural barriers to share the good news with former enemies—with signs and wonders confirming their preaching.

After the publication of the Indian edition of this book I had the privilege of meeting a young Naga leader, Edward Renpi Odyüo. His grandfather-in-law, Chen-o Khuzuthrupa, (from Chenwetnyu Village) had been a headhunter. Edward related how Chen-o's grandfather, a king in the Konyak tribe, had been killed in a raid by men from three other villages. Chen-o and his father organized a raid of vengeance. They killed 120 men in the first village, and were planning to raid the other two villages involved. But before they did Chen-o happened to go to the village of Wakching, where he was confronted by Longri Ao, an evangelist missionary from the Ao tribe. Longri prophesied to him and brought him to faith. This was in the 1950s. Like the skit I saw, Chen-o Khuzuthrupa made the decision to follow the way of Christ rather than seek more vengeance.

Interestingly, this happened in the village of Wakching, which had been visited by C. E. Hunter shortly before he left India.[294] Hunter had been well received, and invited to stay. Edward's grandfather-in-law, still alive in 2022 at age 105, has now celebrated his sixty-third spiritual birthday![295] Interviewed by an ethnographic researcher about his head-hunting tattoos, Chen-o said: "After I accepted my Lord, I began to believe in only one spirit, the Holy Spirit."[296]

A biography of Longri Ao describes how his father, a leader and priest among his Ao tribe, had come to the Lord when Christians prayed for his daughter to be healed. Longri went on to be the first family member to attend school, and then Bible school, and then became a missionary to the Konyak tribe. In 1960, Longri was invited to the World Baptist Alliance conference in Brazil. Just before he left, an old Konyak chief showed up at his door:

> Holding a big dao [type of machete]. The man had recently become a Christian—before that, he had strenuously fought the Christians and opposed Longri's work. But this time the ahng [chief] held out the dao and said, "Before I became a Christian I cut off many heads with this dao. Now my arm is going to fight for Jesus. Take this to the Christian people in America and ask them to pray for me."[297]

As an almost but not quite humorous footnote to this topic, David Murry remembered while he was a student at college in the biggest city in Nagaland, Dimapur:

> [In] 1992, there was a war that broke out between the Konyak and Chang tribes and they were taking heads; in the next room, there were two brothers—one was Konyak and one was Chang—we were friends and nominal Christians. They were watching each other!

But David added immediately, as a comment to show the change in customs that had come earlier to their tribe: "Lothas—not so much—where it's war and they're taking heads."[298] Still, when we speak of Nagas taking the good news to another tribe, it was a case of going to former enemies—people or at least the descendants of people who might have killed one's own ancestors. This makes the power of the gospel shine even brighter!

Acknowledgments

My thanks to: C & SA for nurturing our desire for our Lord to express His power in tangible ways; to B & SH and CS for being the context where I could first experience His Spirit; to MM for asking me to base revival thinking on the Bible; for J & VW for first telling us about the Nagaland Revival.

The interviews were a joint project—the two of us would like to express our deepest thanks to the entire Murry family for opening your hearts and your homes to us and sharing your experiences at such a deep level.

The friendship and advice of RS has been of Barnabas proportions, and KJ and CB have been encouraging throughout this effort. TW has so encouraged us as we've shared these stories with live audiences. JR's hospitality has been invaluable in creating a physical setting where this could come to fruition. L & AH, DW, BN and EP have each invested in this in a tangible way—thank you. Thank you CK for listening to the entire manuscript!

To the wonderfully diverse, "a little bit extreme," and eclectic collection of believers who make up our home churches, we say thanks for your support and the friendship and the common life which sustains us.

We're grateful for those who helped with specific information, cited in footnotes, particularly at the American Baptist History Society archives, and of course thanks to KC for suggesting we check those archives.

Thank you to Yak & Yeti Books for providing some rare volumes. A great big vote of thanks to our initial reviewers: RJM, DE, GB and LS; and to JY and MT for your feedback on the proposal. And, of course, thanks to AC and his team, including CS and TB at Deep River Books.

Endnotes

Introduction

[1] Contemporary English Version, with similar ideas conveyed by the New Living Translation and Good News translation.

[2] Sinai Ministry, *This Is Our Story—GO—A Movement to Pursue the Promise of 10,000 Missionaries* (Dimapur, Nagaland: Heritage Publishing House, 2018), 52.

[3] *This Is Our Story*, 52.

Chapter 1: Surveying the Land

[4] There are a couple of definitions of who is a Naga, as well as what comprises a tribe.

[5] India population: 1.366 billion, https://worldpopulationreview.com/countries, accessed Feb. 19, 2021; Naga figures estimated from prior India censuses.

[6] Nagaland is 6,382 sq. miles (16,527 sq. kilometers); https://web.archive.org/web/20100327142224/http://nagaland.nic.in/profile/aglance.htm, accessed March 11, 2021.

[7] The 1951 census of India recorded 46% of the residents of Nagaland as Christian. This varied greatly by tribe, as one tribe at that point had yet to have a single baptized believer (the Yimchungs).

[8]   R. Vashum. *Indo-Naga Conflict: Problem and Resolution* (New Delhi, India: Indian Social Institute, 2001), 66.

[9]   *This Is Our Story*, 52.

[10]   See J. Edwin Orr, *Evangelical Awakenings in Southern Asia*. (Minneapolis: Bethany Fellowship, 1975).

[11]   The census of India (2011) shows the state of Nagaland as 87.93% Christian. Many of the 12% not professing Christ are from ethnic groups who have moved to the state from elsewhere in India.

[12]   This verse has also been applied to the rebirth of the political nation-state of Israel.

[13]   Jonathan Edwards, *Some Thoughts Concerning the Present Revival of Religion in New England* (1742), https://ccel.org/ccel/edwards/works1/works1.ix.ii.vi.html, 379, accessed March 8, 2021.

Chapter 2: Sowing Seeds in Fallow Ground

[14]   Narola Ao McFayden, *Traveling in Time with Pioneers of Our Faith: Edward Winter Clark and Mary Mead Clark* (North Charleston, SC: CreateSpace, 2016), 99.

[15]   Most, if not all, missionaries touching Nagaland were from the American Baptist Foreign Mission Society. This society decided in 1845 that they couldn't appoint slaveholders to serve as missionaries. This historic decision led to the withdrawal of many churches from the Society and then to the formation of the Southern Baptist Convention.

[16]   The following quotes are taken from the Okotso Baptist Church booklet commemorating their centennial, 1904–2004.

[17]   A town of the Ao tribe of Nagas, where the mission headquarters was located.

[18]   Etisassao would be wonderfully touched in the revival of 1952–54, after he'd been a believer for a half-century. See chapter 14, "How Does Revival Start? (Part II)."

19 This village plays a role in the revival in Okotso in 1952; see chapter 6, "How Does Revival Start?"

20 Longwell's account is from the Okotso Baptist Church booklet commemorating their centennial, 1904–2004, 105–109. His account was edited by a descendant, R. G. Doll.

21 Ibid, 99.

Chapter 3: World War Enters Our Story

22 T. Kikon, foreword in Merithung Mozhui. *A Brief Account of My Personal Testimonies* (Wokha, Nagaland, 1995), i.

23 At a 2013 debate at the British National Army Museum, the combined battle of Kohima-Imphal was voted Britain's greatest battle. Angus Mac-Swan, "Victory over Japanese at Kohima Named Britain's Greatest Battle," Reuters, April 21, 2013, https://www.reuters.com/article/britain-kohima-imphal-nagaland-manipur-w-idINDEE93K04W20130421; accessed March 8, 2021. Imphal is the capital of Manipur, an adjoining state to what is now Nagaland.

24 The British Colonial officer in charge of the Naga Hills area.

25 Jonathan Glancey, *Nagaland—A Journey to India's Forgotten Frontier* (London: Faber and Faber, 2011), 132–133.

26 Words by John Maxwell Edmonds, inspired by the Greek poet Simonides' words on a burial mound at the site of the battle of Thermopylae. Billy Graham would quote the inscription when reporting on his visit to Nagaland in 1972.

27 Glancey, *Nagaland*, 129–130.

28 He tells about the dream after the March-April 1954 dream, so it may have come in between, before his conversion.

29 Merithung was a member of the Lotha tribe; "Lotha Association" would refer to the association of Baptist churches. Although never a leader in this Baptist association, he would play a key role in two different group-

ings of Naga churches, as told in chapter 9, "Do 'a Little Bit Extreme' Remnants Sustain Revival?"

30   Mozhui. *A Brief Account*, 1–2.

31   Ibid.

32   Iain H. Murray. *Revival and Revivalism: The Making and Marring of American Evangelicalism 1750–1858* (Edinburgh, Scotland: The Banner of Truth Trust, 1994), 332; citing J. Edwin Orr, *"The Event of the Century": The 1857–58 Awakening: A Startling Update,* unpublished manuscript.

33   Ibid, 342, 344. New York City was growing rapidly during the period, and the combined population of New York City and Brooklyn in 1860 was more than one million, but fifty thousand would still be a considerable percentage of the city (https://www2.census.gov/library/publications/decennial/1860/population/1860a-26.pdf, accessed June 9, 2021).

34   Ibid, 385; citing J. W. Alexander, *Forty Years' Familiar Letters of James W. Alexander,* Vol. 2, edited by John Hall (New York: Scribner, 1860), 279.

Chapter 4: Revival Happens Personally

35   See chapter 2, "Sowing Seeds in Fallow Ground."

36   Uncle Murry's son-in-law, interview, Oct. 30, 2019. For security reasons his name has been withheld.

37   Rocky Grams, *In Awe in Argentina* (Lake Mary, FL: Creation House, 2006), 101.

Chapter 5: Horror Starts after Revival Begins

38   Pregnant ladies did suffer in particular during the initial military occupation, and there are Nagas who were born in caves during this period because of the destruction of villages.

39 R. Vashum. *Indo-Naga Conflict: Problem and Resolution* (New Delhi, India: Indian Social Institute, 2001), 66. The Assam Rifles are a paramilitary unit having the status of the regular India Army.

40 A referendum organized by and within the Naga tribes May to July 1951 was unanimous (99%) in backing independence. Vashum. *Indo-Naga Conflict,* 37.

41 Ibid, 39.

42 Murray, *Revival and Revivalism,* 380.

43 Ibid, 419; citing *The Presbyterian Magazine,* 1858, 253–54.

44 Jacques Ellul, *Prayer and the Modern Man* (New York: Seabury Press. 1970), 167.

Chapter 6: How Does Revival Start?

45 Jesus makes a wordplay, since the same Greek word, *pneumatos,* can mean "spirit" or "wind."

46 For more discussion on the origins of revival, see chapter 14, "How Does Revival Start? (Part II)."

47 Interview, Chunbeno Murry, translated from Lotha by Ajano Murry, Oct. 8, 2019.

48 Nagaland Christian Revival Church. *Revival Golden Jubilee 1962–2012,* booklet (2012), 5.

49 Ibid.

50 The Greek word for "word" as in "word of Christ" is *rhema*—a specific, particular word—as opposed to *logos,* meaning a general or overall revelation.

Chapter 7: The Fruits of Revival Are Personal

51 L. Yaniethung Murry, tract, Wokha, Nagaland, 1991.

52 For details on the incident, see chapter 16, "Vengeance Is the Lord's."

53   Mozhui, *A Brief Account*, 3–4.

54   Unlike manna which only appeared for six days out of a week!

55   David Murry, interview, Siliguri, West Bengal, Oct. 17, 2019.

56   Mozhui, *A Brief Account*, 5.

57   Peter Kreeft, *Wisdom of the Heart* (Gastonia, NC: TAN Books, 2020), 75.

Chapter 8: Families Pay a Price for Revival

58   One popular Hindu god figure is Ganesh—an elephant's head with a broken tusk on the body of a man.

59   Mozhui, *A Brief Account*, 5.

60   Ibid, 5.

61   Evidently when he said there was "no food" for the children, there was still some food in the house for him to eat something!

62   Mozhui, *A Brief Account*, 9.

63   Ibid.

64   Or more likely the person "has an unclean spirit" or is "demonized."

65   Grams, *In Awe in Argentina*, 114–115.

Chapter 9: Do "a Little Bit Extreme" Remnants Sustain Revival?

66   Nagaland Christian Revival Church, *Revival Golden Jubilee 1962–2012*, 2.

67   Ibid, 3.

68   Ibid, 6.

69   Two different forms of bread found in the Indian subcontinent.

70   Nagaland Christian Revival Church, *Revival Golden Jubilee 1962–2012*, 7.

71   Ibid, 7.

72   ". . . each one was hearing them speak in his own language." Acts 2:6 can

easily be understood to have happened in the same fashion as this incident among the Lothas.

73 English is the official state language of Nagaland.

74 The account appears to say this was the first time Naga believers received the gift of tongues, although this seems unlikely given the level of Holy Spirit activity in various places starting in 1952. But the meeting certainly must have been an important milestone.

75 Nagaland Christian Revival Church, *Revival Golden Jubilee 1962–2012*, 6.

76 Ibid, 3.

77 Ibid, 13.

78 This no doubt refers to the ongoing military operations by the Indian Army. Twice, other Naga believers tried to get Merithung in trouble with the Indian authorities. See chapter 20, "Revival and Division."

79 Nagaland Christian Revival Church, *Revival Golden Jubilee 1962–2012*, 3.

80 Ibid, 3–4.

81 Ibid, 4.

82 India is all one time zone, so sunrise does come quite early on its eastern border.

83 E. Merithung Mozhui, *Chronology of Nagaland Revival*, tract (2002), 3.

84 The Indian Army uses English for internal communication, so all officers would understand it.

85 Nagaland Christian Revival Church, *Revival Golden Jubilee 1962–2012*, 9.

86 Mozhui, *Chronology of Nagaland Revival*, 3–4.

87 The Christian Revival Church would eventually become two denominations.

88 His exact tenure is unclear from the booklet, but apparently Merithung

served two or three years.

89   Assemblies of God in East India, "History of AGEI," https://ageidima-pur.in/index.php/history-of-agei, accessed April 2, 2021.

90   Evidently, even during the restrictions on Westerners visiting Nagaland, Nunn had some access and connection to Nagaland. His son Tommy Nunn remembers: "In the 1960's, a young man named Neuihulie from the Angami tribe came to Southwestern Assemblies of God College (in Waxahachie, Texas) to go to college," which led to David Nunn funding Kohima Bible College. Tommy Nunn, email, March 26, 2021.

91   Bryan Nerren. interview, Shelbyville, TN, Nov. 18, 2020.

Chapter 10: High Tide of the Spirit

92   L. Yaniethung Murry, *O Nagaland* (Wokha, Nagaland: Self-published tract, 1989 and 1991), ii.

93   First wave would be in the 1950s; second wave, 1960s.

94   We recognize any written academic summary of a string of spiritual events loses some of the punch and flavor of a prophetic rendering. We trust the reader can "read between the lines" and appreciate the depth of what was happening.

95   Akümla Longkumer, *Revival in Nagaland—Fact or Fallacy?* (Mokokc-hung, Nagaland: Clark Theological College, 1986), 35; citing Alemmeren.

96   Longkumer, *Revival in Nagaland,* 35.

97   Revival leader and authority J. Edwin Orr was part of getting Graham to visit Nagaland. Interview, Glenn Sheppard, Lees Summit, Missouri, July 1, 2021.

98   Highland Dawn Media, "Rev. Billy Graham's Kohima Crusade 1972!" YouTube video, 4:29, https://www.youtube.com/watch?v=BWWjCES6w9E, accessed Dec. 31, 2020. The video has footage from the visit, showing Graham, the audience, and scenery at different times. There are placards with tribal names, no doubt to guide interpreters and ushers.

99 Worldwide Index of Sermons, "Why We Came to Nagaland—Billy Graham," YouTube video, 11:03, https://www.youtube.com/watch?v=FpEi8vwa54E, accessed Dec. 31, 2020. There are no visuals of Graham; audio track only.

100 In the longer audio version of Graham's ministry report, filmed as part of his ministry communication, Graham says the morning services were at 6:30 am, and the other two services were at 12 noon and 4 pm so they could finish before dark when it got cold. Worldwide Index of Sermons, "Why We Came to Nagaland—Billy Graham."

101 Naga Seminarian, "Who Are the Nagas? Billy Graham on Nagaland (esp. for Nagas in India)," YouTube video, 2:22, https://www.youtube.com/watch?v=Ycj4V_31FiU, accessed Dec. 31, 2020.

102 Ibid.

103 Worldwide Index of Sermons, "Why We Came to Nagaland—Billy Graham.".

104 V. Leno Peseyie-Maase, *God's Glory on Himalaya Mountains* (Maitland, FL: Xulon Press. 2009), 58–59. Angami is a Naga tribe. Attendance figures taken from the 1985 booklet *Great Is Thy Faithfulness* by the Baptist Centenary Publicity Committee, 58.

105 Ibid, 43.

106 The Lothas are a neighboring tribe to the Aos.

107 Longkumer, *Revival in Nagaland,* 36.

108 Ibid; citing *The Nagaland Revival Movement,* Nov. 1, 1984, 37.

109 Ibid, 37.

110 Ibid, 38–40; quoting Ao Temien, *God's Rain* (Mokokchung, Nagaland: Ao C.Y.E. Press, 1979), 12.

111 Ibid, 40.

112 Ibid, 40–42.

113 Ibid, 42.

114 Chewing betelnut is a common stimulant in the Indian subcontinent,

comparable to chewing tobacco in other cultures.

[115]   Personal interview by Ademo Ngullie of Des Short, Siliguri, West Bengal, February 7, 2020.

[116]   Lano Longchar, *The King's Messenger* (Dimapur, Nagaland: Heritage Publishing House, 2014), 34–35.

[117]   Ibid, 35. His name is spelled both "Lanu" and "Lano."

[118]   "And when you hear the sound of marching in the tops of the balsam trees, then rouse yourself, for then the Lord has gone out before you" (2 Samuel 5:25).

[119]   The Murrys' first daughter, Elizabeth, was born in 1965.

[120]   A type of machete.

[121]   "For I know the plans I have for you, declares the Lord, plans for welfare and not for evil, to give you a future and a hope" (Jeremiah 29:11).

[122]   This tribe is a combination of several tribes: "Zeme, Liangmei, Rongmei and Puipei. . . . In social organization, religious, and economic activities and organizations, the Zeliangrongs have very strong common features. The seemingly different dialects spoken by them have linguistic affinity." Ramkhun Pamei, *The Zeliangrong Nagas: A Study of Tribal Christianity* (New Delhi: Uppal Publishing House. 1996), 5. The tribe lives in three different states: Nagaland, Manipur, and Assam.

[123]   In other words, "outsiders" to the community, as police are often assigned from other districts.

[124]   Pamei, *The Zeliangrong Nagas,* 75.

[125]   City Population, "Manipur,"https://www.citypopulation.de/en/india/manipur, accessed Jan. 18, 2021.

[126]   Kairingam Pamai, interview, Siliguri, West Bengal. October 2018.

[127]   Census of India figures, from https://en.wikipedia.org/wiki/Christianity_in_Nagaland#Trends, accessed Jan. 18, 2021.

[128]   Author's estimate. Census figures show no Christians in 1941, while the 1931 census showed 12.8%.

129 Census of India figures, from https://en.wikipedia.org/wiki/Christianity_in_Nagaland#Trends, accessed Jan. 18, 2021. Nagaland has become more ethnically diverse during the past decades, with people from other states moving in. This may explain a slight decline in 2011 to 87.93% following the peak percentage claiming Christianity as coming in 2001 at 89.97%.

130 Longkumer, *Revival in Nagaland,* 43. Longri Ao, former General Secretary of the Nagaland Baptist Church Council, July 10, 1978, letter to former American Baptist missionary to Nagaland, Bengt Anderson.

131 Ibid, 91–92; citing *World Christianity, South Asia,* vol. 3, 1981.

132 Ibid, 94. These would be churches recognized by the Nagaland Baptist General Council, so this figure wouldn't include other groups like the revival churches.

133 Ibid.

134 Ibid.

135 Sinai Ministry, *This Is Our Story,* 20.

136 Ibid, 21.

137 Henri J. M. Nouwen, *In the Name of Jesus* (New York: Crossroad. 1989), 48–49.

Chapter 11: After Revival: Judgment or Wilderness?

138 Chumbeno Murry, Oct. 8, 2019, as translated from Lotha by her niece Ajano Murry.

139 Thungbemo and Mhono Murry, joint interview, Wokha, Nagaland, Oct. 10, 2019.

140 David Murry, interview, Siliguri, West Bengal, Oct. 17, 2019.

141 Ibid.

142 See chapter 15, "The Severe Hand of God," for details.

143 Elizabeth did marry Lambert Odyüo and raised a family. He died in 2020.

144   Ralph Mahoney's focus was equipping indigenous church leaders through training. His book *The Shepherd's Staff* helped many leaders in the developing world.

145   In Assam, a bordering state to Nagaland.

146   David Murry, interview, Siliguri, West Bengal, Oct. 17, 2019.

147   Worldwide Index of Sermons, "Why We Came to Nagaland—Billy Graham." Italics added for emphasis.

Chapter 12: Trying to Walk Godly in Babylon

148   Hutton said that after the Battle of Kohima not one house remained standing in the entire city. Twelve thousand dwellings needed to be rebuilt in the district, which included the city.

149   This reference to Great Britain as the "protecting power" rings tragic, given the British decision to keep Nagaland under New Delhi's control.

150   M. Alemchiba, *A Brief Historical Account of Nagaland* (Kohima, Nagaland: Naga Institute of Culture, 1970), 135–137.

151   Glancey, *Nagaland*, 106. Glancey describes Hutton as one of "the fiercest critics of the work of missions."

152   See chapter 18, "Weeds: Part of the Harvest."

153   Mhono and Ajano Murry, joint interview, Wokha, Nagaland, Oct. 8, 2019.

154   Murry, *O Nagaland*, 8–10. More on this in chapter 18, "Weeds: Part of the Harvest."

155   A reference to how accepting New Delhi's money stymied the independence movement.

156   The central government of India has poured money into Nagaland essentially to buy the loyalty of the Naga people. One businessman the interviewers met gave a specific example of the corruption he encountered in government leaders, which was telling in more ways than one. The state legislative body (assembly) was buying tires sometime

in 2010s. They asked the tire dealer to mark up the price 30% and then return that 30% to the legislators as a kickback. The tire dealer wanted to show integrity, so he said he would give them a "gift" of 5% out of his normal retail markup, but he wouldn't charge more than the manufacturer's suggested retail price. The legislative body bought their tires elsewhere.

Chapter 13: Mission: One Fruit of Revival

157 Melli (also spelled Malli) is one of the few towns in India to overlap state borders. Part is in West Bengal, part in Sikkim, on the Teesta River.

158 David Murry, interview, Siliguri, West Bengal, Oct. 17, 2019.

159 The Centre for Policy Studies (a Hindu nationalist think-tank based in Chennai, India) gives the census figures cited: https://blog.cpsindia.org/2016/09/religion-data-of-census-2011-xxix.html, accessed March 28, 2021.

160 *Latter Rain Revival Ministry's Newsletter,* Dec. 92–Jan. 93, 10–11.

161 Namchi is high enough in altitude to have daily lows of 45 degrees Fahrenheit in January. Few houses have furnaces or central heat.

162 *Latter Rain Revival Ministry's Newsletter,* Dec. 92–Jan. 93, 13.

163 Ibid, 15–16.

164 There are and have been various groups seeking independence or autonomy from the central government of India besides the Nagaland independence movement. This man was part of the Ghurka movement, trying to establish some autonomy for Nepali people groups in Sikkim and the northern part of West Bengal.

165 David Mangratee is credited with popularizing the Christian greeting *Jaimasi* (Victory to Messiah) as an alternative to the Hindi greeting *Namaste*, which means: "I worship the god in you."

166 Started under David Nunn's sponsorship, who had also been involved in the orphanage Merithung managed for some time.

167   One-sixth of Bhutan's residents were forced out during the period lead-
      ing up to the early 1990s to quash appeals for democracy and more
      rights for Nepali-speaking residents. Maximillian Mørch, "Bhutan's
      Dark Secret: The Lhotshampa Expulsion," *The Diplomat*, Sept. 21, 2016,
      https://thediplomat.com/2016/09/bhutans-dark-secret-the-lhot-
      shampa-expulsion, accessed Jan. 25, 2021.

168   A dish common in India, made of lentils.

169   The letter continues on in the same way and includes some other family
      news, and closes "Your ever loving, Mhono."

170   See chapter 16, "Vengeance Is the Lord's," for details of that ordeal.

171   Prabha Baraik, interview, Dec. 11, 2020.

172   Ibid.

173   Ibid.

174   Deepak Kuswar, interview, Siliguri, West Bengal, Feb. 19, 2020.

175   Deepak Kuswar, interview, Siliguri, West Bengal, Oct. 30, 2019.

176   Ajano Vaders, interview, Siliguri, West Bengal, April 17, 2022.

177   Interview with former student, 2020.

178   Ajano Vaders, interview, Siliguri, West Bengal, April 23, 2022.

179   One instructor has likened the course to a cross between a Youth with
      a Mission six-month Discipleship Training School and a conventional
      Bible college.

Chapter 14: How Does Revival Start? (Part II)

180   The Kohima district is home to the Angami tribe.

181   Merithung Mozhui, *Chronology of Nagaland Revival,* tract (2002), 3–4.

182   Longkumer, *Revival in Nagaland,* 27; quoting Ao Temien, *God's Rain,* 12.

183   Ibid, 27. The Impur mission station was a few miles from Mokokchung,
      an important town of the Ao tribe.

184 Ibid, 1; quoting Rikum Ao, *Nagaland Revival, 1952.*

185 Aerogram letters were a piece of stationery, smaller than an 8 ½ x 11 piece of paper, sold by a country's postal service as a self-contained mailer.

186 C. E. Hunter, aerogram letter to Dr. H. E. Hinton, American Baptist Foreign Missions Society, dated April 12, 1948, from C .E. Hunter files in the American Baptist Historical Society archives, Mercer University, Atlanta. Caps in original.

187 Longkumer, *Revival in Nagaland,* 28–29.

188 Ibid, 29. Note that work among other tribes was with former enemies, in a different language.

189 Ibid, 29.

190 C. E. Hunter, *1950 Impur Field Report,* hand-dated Dec. 21, 1950; from C. E. Hunter files in the American Baptist Historical Society archives, Mercer University, Atlanta.

191 Ibid. The number he reports saved matches the number he reports as water baptized that year.

192 McFayden, *Traveling in Time,* 68–69.

193 Findagrave.com, accessed Jan. 8, 2020. The ship's physician gives the cause of death as coronary thrombosis.

194 Cleda Hunter letter to J. E. Skoglund, dated Jan. 31, 1951. From C .E. Hunter files in the American Baptist Historical Society archives, Mercer University, Atlanta. Sangtam is another Naga tribe and language.

195 Longkumer, *Revival in Nagaland,* 30–31.

196 T. L. Osborn, *Frontier Evangelism: God's Indispensable Method of World Evangelism* (Tulsa, OK: T. L. Osborn, 1955), 34–35. He also talks about this in *Healing the Sick* (Tulsa, OK: Harrison House, 1992; original 1951), 42–43. He went to India in 1945 as a 21-year-old.

197 Ladonna Osborn, email, Jan. 6, 2021.

198 Both cities, interestingly, would be consistent with Osborn's experience, as both have large Muslim populations. Muslims are a minority in

India as a whole, but still have a large presence in some cities—and due to India's large population, the country has the second-highest number of Muslims of any nation.

199 *The Shepherd's Staff* is a basic pastoral manual developed by Ralph Mahoney for distribution in the majority world. David Murry now has his father's copy.

200 Mark Buntain was based in Kolkata, and founded a hospital, mercy ministry, and churches there. He died in June 1989.

201 Okotso Baptist Church booklet commemorating their centennial, 1904–2004, 101–102.

202 The same man who was threatened with death by other villagers when missionary R. B. Longwell attempted to visit the village; see chapter 2, "Sowing Seeds in Fallow Ground."

203 Okotso Baptist Church booklet commemorating their centennial, 1904–2004, 99.

204 Ibid, 98.

205 Murray. *Revival and Revivalism,* 380; citing George A. Blackburn, *The Life Work of John L. Girardeau* (Columbia, SC: The State Company, 1916), 100–101.

Chapter 15: The Severe Hand of God

206 Murry, *O Nagaland,* ii.

207 Contemporary students of culture will distinguish between cultures based on guilt/innocence (most Western cultures), shame/honor (many Asian cultures), fear/power, and purity/pollution.

208 Murry, tract, *O Nagaland,* 1991, p. 18.

209 This wording would be typical, particularly for his generation, since Nagas don't see themselves as part of India.

210 Murry, *O Nagaland,* n.p.

211   L. Yaniethung Murry, *Revival Ministry in the Himalayan Four Corner Courts,* self-published tract (Siliguri, India, hand-dated April 1994), 1.

212   Murry, *O Nagaland,* ii.

213   Murry, *Revival Ministry in the Himalayan Four Corner Courts,* 8.

214   Ibid, 9.

Chapter 16: Vengeance Is the Lord's

215   David Murry, interview, Siliguri, West Bengal, Oct. 17, 2019.

216   Ibid.

217   My thanks to Andy Crouch for pointing out my imbalanced view. Andy Crouch, "The Return of Shame," *Christianity Today,* March 2015, Vol. 59, No. 2, 32, http://andy-crouch.com/articles/the_return_of_shame, accessed March 10, 2021.

Chapter 17: Suffering: Soil or Fertilizer for Revival?

218   Vashun, *Indo-Naga Conflict,* 65; quoting Tanjenyuba Ao, *British Occupation Naga Country* (Mokokchung: Naga Literature Society. 1993), 289.

219   Available for free download at https://asiaharvest.org/free-ebooks. Any reader interested in the topic of revival should read it as well. Hattaway looks at the history through many other sources. This move of God is so vast that it needs more than one account.

220   Equivalent at that time to twelfth grade in the United States.

221   The comprehensive listing of Christian martyrs in *World Christian Trends AD 30–AD 2200* by David Barrett and Todd Johnson (Pasadena, CA: William Carey, 2001), 244, reported 300,000 total deaths between 1947 and 1999 in Nagaland, and classified ten thousand as martydoms. Their total death figure is higher than other reports.

222   Mhono, Thungbemo and Serena Murry, interview, Wokha, Nagaland, Oct. 10, 2019. The incident was in 1984 or 1985.

223   Vashun, *Indo-Naga Conflict,* 69. These two entries are in a long list, taken from various sources.

224   Mhono, Thungbemo and Serena Murry, interview, Wokha, Nagaland, Oct. 10, 2019.

225   See chapter 20, "Revival and Division."

Chapter 18: Weeds: Part of the Harvest

226   James Montgomery Boice, *The Minor Prophets, Vol. 2* (Grand Rapids, MI: Baker Books, 1986), 375.

227   Murry, *O Nagaland.* (His father-in-law Merithung Mozhui would express similar concerns in his 1995 booklet.)

228   Ibid, 1–3.

229   Ibid, 4.

230   Boldface in original for emphasis.

231   A general term for elected government officials in India—so this isn't referring to church leaders.

232   The capital of the state of Nagaland. The legislative body is called an assembly, so "assembly house" refers to their meeting place.

233   Murry, *O Nagaland,* 7.

234   Ibid, 8.

235   Peseyie-Maase. *God's Glory on Himalaya Mountains,* 108.

236   Murry, *O Nagaland,* 11–12.

237   Ibid, 13–14.

238   Alan Murry, interview, Siliguri, West Bengal, Oct. 28, 2019.

239   Sinai Ministry, "This Is Our Story," YouTube video, posted Oct. 3, 2018, 8:42, https://www.youtube.com/watch?v=fYye16n65TQ, accessed Jan. 8, 2021.

Chapter 19: How Does Abundant Life Work?

240   A *pai* is one-hundredth of a rupee.

Chapter 20: Revival and Division

241   A *panchayat* is similar to a mayor.

242   Okotso Baptist Church booklet commemorating their centennial, 1904–2004. 101.

243   The Nagaland Christian Revival Church booklet's description of the teaching differences have already been quoted in chapter 9, "Do 'a Little Bit Extreme' Remnants Sustain Revival?" Here's the full description the Revival Church gives of the difference: "The Revival people started practicing water baptism of the believers after being revived, defying the earlier baptism they had without repentance or being saved. They understood that water baptism without genuine repentance was of no use rather it was an error to be rectified. This was outrageously opposed by the then church leaders." Nagaland Christian Revival Church booklet, 4.

244   Okotso Baptist Church booklet commemorating their centennial, 1904–2004. 102.

245   Ibid.

246   David Murry, interview, Siliguri, West Bengal, Oct. 17, 2019.

247   Although the quotation is often attributed to Augustine of Hippo, the first official record of it is by a Lutheran writer, Rupertus Meldenius, https://faculty.georgetown.edu/jod/augustine/quote.html, accessed April 30, 2021.

Chapter 21: Where Does New Wine Fit?

248   The group who run the first structure (the time-limited training class) may be a second structure (a team or society themselves).

249   Obviously believers, whether a training class or mission society, are all part of "the church." Someone might quibble that I'm restricting the

term "church" when I use it this way. Nevertheless this is the way the term is used in normal conversation, when "churches" are contrasted with "parachurch ministries." It would be helpful to change our language to contrast "congregations" and "ministries."

250 Christian Revival Church, Nagaland Christian Revival Church, and Assemblies of God. The Assemblies of God existed outside Nagaland as a denomination decades before the revival in Nagaland; but their presence in Nagaland was because of the revival.

251 Note that the Chathe Prayer Center is featured in the Nagaland Christian Revival Church's report given later in the chapter.

252 *Find Us Faithful,* published in 2017 and celebrating twenty-five years history of their ministry, says the couple observed ten days of fasting at the Chathe prayer center and that the word to go to Sikkim came on the ninth day; 5.

253 At this point in his life Uncle Murry must have been part of a local church fellowship.

254 L. Yaniethung Murry, recording, March 8, 2019.

255 Darjeeling district is the northernmost district of the state of West Bengal, India and includes the city of Siliguri.

256 This refers to the directional word Uncle Murry received from the Lord, leading him to the "four corner courts of the Himalayas": Nepal, Sikkim, Bhutan and Darjeeling district.

257 Nagaland Christian Revival Church, *Revival Golden Jubilee 1962–2012,* booklet (2012), 21.

258 Ibid.

259 "Inmates" are evidently not "full-time." The term probably describes short-term residents, which would include drug addicts going through recovery.

260 Nagaland Christian Revival Church. *Revival Golden Jubilee,* 23.

261 Ibid, 23.

262 My thanks to the late Floyd McClung, founder of All Nations Family; and Adam Cox, a pastor at Navah Church in Kansas City, for these two questions. *Navah* is a Hebrew verb meaning "to bring home and make beautiful."

Chapter 23: The Choice of Zeal: Burning Out Rather Than Rusting

263 Eliza Edmunds Hewitt, "Will There Be Any Stars?" Shut in because of a spinal malady, she started writing poems for her church. https://hymnary.org/text/i_am_thinking_today_of_that_beautiful_la, accessed May 12, 2022.

264 Cleda Hunter letter to J. E. Skoglund, dated Jan. 31, 1951. From C. E. Hunter files in the American Baptist Historical Society archives, Mercer University, Atlanta.

265 Uncle Murry's son-in-law, interview, India, Oct. 30, 2019.

266 Prashant Thapa, interview, Darjeeling, West Bengal, Nov. 6, 2019.

267 *Latter Rain Revival Ministry's Newsletter,* Dec. 92–Jan. 93, 5. The quotation is from "Until Then" by Stuart Hamblen.

Chapter 24: Concluding Thoughts

268 Uncle Murry's son-in-law, interview, April 4, 2021.

269 Lano Longchar, *The King's Messenger* (Dimapur, Nagaland: Heritage Publishing House, 2014), 35.

270 Ibid, 36.

271 Charles Spurgeon, *Morning and Evening,* July 9, https://www.ccel.org/ccel/spurgeon/morneve.d0709am.html, accessed May 12, 2022.

272 Bill Johnson, pastor, Bethel Church, Redding, CA, "English—The Outpouring," Watchmen for the Nations, YouTube video, May 28, 2020, 4:32:15, https://www.youtube.com/watch?v=QqJwrL2a8Xk, accessed Jan. 13, 2021; quoting Charles Spurgeon (1:13:30).

Appendix 1: Mission: The Fruit Which Brings Revival

273   I recognize that suggesting something is impossible for God is unsound, and that the writer quoted should have simply emphasized that God has chosen to bless unity.

274   F. S. Downs, *The Mighty Works of God: A Brief History of the Council of Baptist Churches in North East India: The Mission Period 1836–1950* (Gauhati: Christian Literature Centre, 1971), 226–227; quoted in Sinai Ministry, *This Is Our Story*, 42.

275   Krishna is the name of one of the key Hindu gods.

276   Nagaland Christian Revival Church. *Revival Golden Jubilee 1962–2012*, 13.

277   David Murry, interview, Siliguri, West Bengal, Oct. 17, 2019.

278   Uncle Murry's son-in-law, interview, Oct. 30, 2019.

279   Ibid.

280   Yaniethung, Mhono, Ajano Murry and a training center graduate, interview, Wokha, Nagaland, Oct. 9, 2019.

Appendix 2: Another Wave?

281   Melissa Steffan, "The Surprising Countries Most Missionaries are Sent From and Go To," *Christianity Today*, July 25, 2013, https://www.christianitytoday.com/news/2013/july/missionaries-countries-sent-received-csgc-gordon-conwell.html, accessed May 12, 2022.

282   Because of the secrecy surrounding the military occupation, the figure is uncertain. Glancey, *Nagaland*, 2, estimates 200,000 deaths from the 1950s through 2010.

283   Sinai Ministry. *This Is Our Story*, 45–46. The comment about "not because your church/parents wants you to go" may be a reference that culturally there's now an expectation that one child out of a Naga family will be dedicated to some form of ministry, not necessarily mission work.

284   Ibid, 46.

285 "Nagaland Missions Movement—History," https://www.nbcc-naga-land.org/nagalandmissionsmovement, accessed Jan. 8, 2021.

286 "Nagaland Missions Movement," https://www.nbcc-nagaland.org, accessed Jan. 8, 2021.

287 Peseyie-Maase. *God's Glory on Himalaya Mountains,* 159. The reference labels the missionaries as "local missionaries," so it's unclear if all would qualify as going cross-culturally, but certainly her brother did, as he went to Sikkim.

288 Highland Dawn Media, "'Go Nagaland' with Tali Angh & Sinai Ministry at Kohima," YouTube video, posted April 23, 2019, 2:32:50, https://www.youtube.com/watch?v=FXEiIssd8wI&t=4s, accessed Jan. 8, 2021.

289 Ibid.

Appendix 3: What about Head-Hunting?

290 C. E. Hunter. 1948 Annual Report, Impur, Assam, from C. E. Hunter files in the American Baptist Historical Society archives, Mercer University, Atlanta. Caps in original.

291 C. E. Hunter, May 6, 1950 letter to J. E. Skoglund, secretary of the American Baptist Foreign Missions Board. from C.E. Hunter files in the American Baptist Historical Society archives, Mercer University, Atlanta.

292 National Geographic, "Why These Headhunters Converted to Christianity," YouTube video, 3:39, https://www.youtube.com/watch?v=oLs-UoqzLlU, accessed Oct. 22, 2020.

293 Ibid.

294 "Rev. Longri: The First Missionary to Konyak Land" YouTube video, 7:22, https://www.youtube.com/watch?v=-oBRzdoqbc4, accessed May 22, 2022.

295 Edward Renpi Odyuo, interview, Dimapur, Nagaland, May 2, 2022.

296 Lars Krutak, "To Mark with the Tattoo: Chen-Naga Tiger Spirit Tattoos and Indigenous Ontologies in Northeast India," in *Tattooed Bodies,* James Martell and Erik Larsen, eds. (Cham, Switzerland: Springer Nature), 108.

297 Richard G. Beers, *Walk the Distant Hills* (New York: Friendship Press. 1969), 11–12, 62.

298 David Murry, interview, Siliguri, West Bengal, Oct. 17, 2019.

Printed in the United States
by Baker & Taylor Publisher Services